In His Marvelous Love,

Whisper Jesus

Rev. Rebecca A. Keefe

Rev. Rebecca Ann Keefe

Whisper Jesus (Book)

Dove "Faith-Friendly"

For All Ages

SLVDNO

Content Rating Descriptions

Synopsis

What is "Whisper Jesus" all about? It is a collection of sacred poems on biblical characters and circumstances, based entirely on Scripture, that encourages the reader to stop and simply whisper the name of Jesus.

Dove Review

"Whisper Jesus" is a book of poems and devotions, written by Rebecca Ann Keefe. It is very inspirational, reverent and encouraging.

For example, in the devotion titled "Free Indeed," Rebecca writes about God forgetting about our sins after He has forgiven us. She also includes Scripture verses. This truth gives us great freedom. She also reminds the reader to forgive others, as well. God chooses not to remember, and we should do the same. She writes that we should simply whisper, "Jesus, thank you!" She uses Jeremiah 31:34, which says that God remembers our sins no more. She adds her poem, "Free Indeed," with the devotion, and she writes of the covenants of God with Abraham, David, and us.

This 283-page book includes devotions with titles such as "Button your lip!" and "Love Revealed." Her topics range from how we can give up struggles to God, which she writes about in "Palms Up," to how we would live in our home if we pictured Jesus as our guest, sitting across the table from us.

We are pleased to present this book our "Faith-Friendly" Seal for all ages, although it is not targeted toward very young readers. In the devotion, "God, Do You Care?" she addresses God in the midst of trials, and it will encourage every reader -as will this entire book. We present it five Doves, and that's our highest rating. Read it, and be encouraged and blessed!

Content Description Info

Sex: None **Language:** None **Violence:** None **Drugs:** None **Nudity:** None

Reviewer: Edwin L. Carpenter
Source: Book
Company: Abba Father Media, Inc.
Writer: Rebecca Keefe Genre: Devotional Pages:283

<u>Dedication</u>

This book is dedicated to my mother, Adeline Columba Ciavatta Rice who went to be with the Lord in 2005. She was not only my Mom, but my prayer partner, my confidant and my very good friend. Her steadfast love for God and His Word was an example for her six children. Her words often ring loud and clear in my memory, "Becky, have you prayed about it?" As well her admonition to, "just whisper the Name of Jesus," no matter what the issue. To my mother I say, "Though you are in the presence of Jesus – I still miss you. This book is for you Mama."

Whisper Jesus

ACKNOWLEDGEMENTS III

DEDICATION.. IV

"JUST WHISPER – JESUS"... 1

A CITY OF PROMISE AND ENEMIES... 5

A FRESH VISION 8

A HEART TO KNOW HIM 10

A LITTLE CHILD SINGS SWEETLY.. 13

A PRAYER – LOSING A LOVED ONE 15

BATTLES 18

BEFORE – BUT NOW... 21

BUTTON YOUR LIP.. 25

COLD DARK PLACE.. 27

DISAPPOINTMENT VS. HIS APPOINTMENT 30

DOES GOD EVER MAKE MISTAKES 33

ENDURING FAITH 37

FIXING MY EYES UPON JESUS.. 41

FREE INDEED 44

FORGIVENESS.. 47

FRAGRANCE VS. STENCH 50

GET RID OF THE BAGGAGE!... 54

GOD DO YOU CARE?... 56

GOD'S FAIRNESS 61

GOD'S LOVE 66

GRACE UPON GRACE.. 68

HANGING ON OR LETTING GO..71

HAPPY NEW YEAR 73

HE BROUGHT US OUT 75

I AM AMAZED 78

I WONDER...80

IF I COULD PICTURE JESUS..83

IF I COULD TURN BACK TIME 86

IF I WERE KING FOR THE DAY 89

IN HIM 91

IS IT KIND – IS IT NECESSARY – IS IT TRUE?.............................94

IT'S A BEAUTIFUL DAY IN THE NEIGHBORHOOD..........................97

IT'S ALL ABOUT YOU 100

IT'S CHRISTMAS TIME AGAIN 103

JESUS IS THE REASON..106

JOY AND PEACE..109

LEGACY 111

LET GO AND LET GOD 116

LISTEN – LOOK – BELIEVE 118

LIVE IT – ACT IT – NO COMPLAINING......................................122

LOOKING AT ANOTHER NEW YEAR..124

LOOKING FOR LOVE 128

LOOKING THROUGH A GLASS DARKLY 131

LORD I CONFESS...133

LORD TEACH ME YOUR WAYS 136

LORD, YOU ARE SO WORTHY 139

LOVE REVEALED 141

MOSAIC 143

NEVER AGAIN.. 146

NEW COVENANT IN CHRIST JESUS.. 148

NO FISHING ALLOWED 151

NOT WORTHY BUT GRATEFUL... 153

O LORD BE WITH US TODAY 156

OUR THOUGHTS VS HIS THOUGHTS 158

PALMS UP!.. 161

PRAYERS – VS – PRAY-ERS 163

PUZZLE PIECE 167

RECOUNTING 170

REDEEMED.. 173

REFLECT – REMEMBER – REPENT 176

RISE UP AND BELIEVE!.. 179

SECRETS 182

SEEDS.. 185

THE STORY OF THE RUBBER BAND SNAP BACK INTO FOCUS! 188

SOMETIMES, LORD.. 190

STOP! LOOK! LISTEN! 192

STORIES OF LOVE 195

STRENGTH FOR THE JOURNEY... 198

THE BUS 201

THE POINTER.. 204

THE VALLEY OF BACA (WEEPING) 207

THE WALLS..212

THE WEDDING FEAST OF THE LAMB......................216

THEY CAME TO JESUS...219

THINGS HAVEN'T CHANGED...224

THIS IS THE DAY..227

THIS ONE THING I KNOW..229

THOUGHTING - FOR MOTHER'S DAY.............................233

'THOUGHTING' AGAIN ABOUT A FUNERAL.....................235

TO GOD BE THE GLORY...238

WATCHFUL WAITING...241

WE NEVER KNOW..243

WHAT I CAN DO FOR YOU...246

WHAT IS A MOTHER?..249

WHEN I COULDN'T LOVE MYSELF..................................252

WHEN I THINK ABOUT THE CROSS................................255

WHO OR WHAT IS KING...259

WITHIN THIS CIRCLE...262

WORDS...265

WHO IS THIS?...268

YOU MAKE ALL THINGS WORK TOGETHER.....................270

BIBLIOGRAPHY/REFERENCE..273

THANK YOU!...274

ABOUT THE AUTHOR..276

The following poem Whisper Jesus inspired the name of this book.

<u>"Just Whisper – Jesus"</u>

"Just whisper the Name of Jesus" were words said to me by my mom. If I was frightened or afraid this was the encouragement I received. My mom would tell me that the Name of Jesus would put to flight any harm or evil that would try to hinder me. I have found those words to be a comfort and a reminder that I have a Friend who is closer than a brother in the form of my loving Savior and Redeemer. My Grandma Rice (who used to minister alongside of my Grandpa James Rice) used to preach about putting our sins and shortcomings under the blood of Jesus and being covered in His blood. She related it was much like the children of Israel who were protected from the death angel plague of Egypt when the Israelites were instructed to take the blood of a pure lamb and spread it over the doorposts of their homes and when the plague passed over Egypt in the time of Pharaoh all the firstborn were killed except those whose door posts were covered in the blood of the lamb. (Exciting reading in Exodus – Chapters 11 & 12). She constantly taught us if we were covered in the blood of Jesus we would be protected from harm, evil and hurt. There used to be phrase used in Pentecostal circles years ago, "Just plead the Blood of Jesus" which in essence meant to claim the protection and cleansing that is in the Blood of Jesus.

There have been times in my life when I "thought" I had put something "under the blood of Jesus" when, in fact, I had merely swept it under the rug. Mom would say, "Just whisper the name of Jesus, Becky. He'll be there with you. He'll calm your fears, and take away the anxiety and help you work through the hard places." These are words of wisdom, but also from God's precious Word. Words of Jesus in Luke 4:18 The Spirit of the Lord is upon me, because he hath anointed me to preach the gospel to the poor; he hast sent me to heal the brokenhearted, to preach deliverance to the captives, and recovering of sight to the blind, to set at liberty them that are bruised.

So let me encourage you to whisper the Name of Jesus, softly and quietly perhaps, and come to Him with any anxiety, heartbreak or fear. See for yourself how sweet our Lord is and how healing it is to sit in His presence as you totally "Let Go and Let God" take control of your life.

My prayer today is simply: "Heavenly Father, we love You and thank You that You have made provision for us through Your son Jesus Christ. Look at our hearts and our lives today Lord. Help us to live in such a way that it pleases You, and help us sort through the "junk" that is many times slung our way. Even though we may not understand the circumstances that surround us, help us to lean on You and trust in You to do the healing. You are, indeed, the miracle worker, and we ask for the miracle of faith to believe that You do all things well. Help us to just stop, find a quiet place, and simply whisper the sweet name of Jesus. Closing ourselves in with You and You alone. And as we whisper the precious name of Jesus, focusing on You, we are confident that You will whisper back to us. In the sweet name of Jesus our Lord, who is King of kings and Lord of lords, Amen"

Blessings to you! Whisper Jesus in your travels. :-)
October 29, 2013

Whisper Jesus

You spoke to Samuel in a whisper
As You called his name in the night
You spoke to Elijah softly
As you showed him all your might

You spoke peace to winds and waves
In a boat filled with crying and fear
You spoke to Mary's quiet heart
As the angel of God drew near

Sometimes I don't look for a whisper
I look for a clear loud sound
I don't hear your whisper to my heart
As I run here and there and around

I find it hard to quiet myself
Lord sweep over my Spirit, sweet Friend
You weren't in the thunder and lightning
In the earthquake, the fire, the wind

But you spoke to Elijah in a quiet voice
And you told him not to fear
Hiding from those who chased him
You whispered as You drew near

You showed him You were with him
That he was not alone as he thought
There were many others in the race

Whisper Jesus

All his work was not for naught

You whisper Peace to our ailing hearts
At wits end you give a song
Bringing hope and rest and encouragement
As we travel on roads that are long

Help me Lord, to hear Your whisper
Softly whispering Your Name in prayer
Whispering "Jesus" "Jesus" "Jesus"
Casting on You my worries and care

I'll whisper Your Name softly
For Your whisper I'll listen too
I'll quiet my heart in stillness
As you love me and I'll love you

Make it so, Lord Jesus
Help me hear Your still small voice

Rebecca A. Keefe
August 23, 2013

A City of Promise and Enemies

Fresh beginnings, promises fulfilled, and enemies, that's pretty much what the book of Nehemiah is all about. It also rings true for our everyday lives as well. We come to God with a new beginning. We see things from a different perspective. Then the trials start. Things go wrong. We are lied to, lied about, deceived. Does that sound familiar? We often have the idea that once we become Christians, accepting Christ as our Savior, we will be trouble free. We are guilt free, redeemed, born fresh and new in our spirit, but we are not free from trials. All we need to do is look at the prophets, the leaders, the disciples, those who followed Jesus. They were transformed, but not trouble free. The story of Nehemiah is a wonderful example of perseverance and dedication, as well as determination to do God's Will. But he had some enemies named Sanballat and Tobiah and others. They looked like the real thing, real friends at first, but they were troublemakers from the start. We too have enemies whose names may not be Sanballat and Tobiah, but they are enemies of the Cross. We too need to be encouraged to hold steady and keep on working in the spirit of Christ. The only way we can do a work for Christ is to keep Him ever most in our heart and mind. Simply Whisper Jesus and it changes our focus. Let me encourage you to do that right now, today. Whisper Jesus.

Nehemiah 4:6 – 9 (NLT)

At last the wall was completed to half its original height around the entire city, for the people had worked very hard.
But when Sanballat and Tobiah and the Arabs, Ammonites, and Ashdodites heard that the work was going ahead and that the gaps in the wall were being repaired, they became furious.

They all made plans to come and fight against Jerusalem and to bring about confusion there.

But we prayed to our God and guarded the city day and night to protect ourselves.

A City of Promise and Enemies

A city of promise
Fresh beginnings and all
A chance for renewal
And rebuilding a wall

The Temple, brought to order
Once the wall was again secured
New courage to begin again
After much trouble was endured

A time of repentance
A time of vowing to do better
A time of choosing sides
Following God's laws by the letter

Yet there will always be those
Who will despise and disdain
Who will try to discourage
Make God's work seem in vain

Sanballat and Tobiah
And others we could name
Came against Nehemiah
Yet, pretended to be the same

Whisper Jesus

Enemies who loved pretending
That they were his closest friends
Appearing to be loyal
But very evil in the end

And, we, like Nehemiah
Need to keep our enemies at bay
By listening to the Word of God
By being watchful as we pray

Still we ask for Your courage, Lord
To fight, or build or meet a need
To recognize we have an enemy
We have You to help us succeed

Nehemiah reminds us again
When in trouble we need to pray
It is Your Grace and Mercy
That will always lead the way.

Thank You that You forgive us
For second chances we give you praise
You hear our cry, wipe the slate clean
It's to You our hands we raise.

Thank you Jesus!

Rebecca A. Keefe
June 12, 2012

A Fresh Vision

Sometimes we lose sight of the Lord. It may not be intentional. It may just be that life as we know it gets in the way. We can become so involved with the urgency of the moment that we simply forget to quiet ourselves and stop for a break. This is when we realize something is missing. This is one of those times we can just sit quietly and Whisper the sweet Name of Jesus. How do we do that? Simple, we just stop. Stop running, stop planning, stop going, going, going. When we finally decide to stop and be quiet I guarantee you will begin to see that you need a fresh vision of Jesus. And when we spend time in His presence our mind will be renewed. Just like this poem says - a fresh vision. Try Whispering Jesus today asking for a fresh vision of Him to be revealed to your heart.

Romans 12:2 (NIV)

....but be transformed by the renewing of your mind. Then you will be able to test and approve what God's will is – his good, pleasing and perfect will.

A Fresh Vision

Lord,
I need a fresh vision
of who Jesus is
and who He is not

A true revelation to
my heart of what
is real and what is rot

Whisper Jesus

Open my eyes, also my mind
With a heart that's
turned towards God

So I can learn
As I study the Word
The path that others have trod

Dropping my perceptions
And misconceptions
Dropping my biases and fear

You, dropping in my heart
A revelation of Jesus
That is solid and clear

Let me have an
'aha' moment
As I live in the world each day

Discerning by Your Spirit
If it's true or false
Should I keep it or throw it away

Lord,
I need a fresh vision
of who Jesus is
and who He is not

Rebecca A. Keefe
September 11, 2012

A Heart To Know Him

We can never have a heart that knows the Lord if we refuse to spend time in His presence. God always rescued His children when they called to Him and when they had decided that His way was best. As they turned to Him, He gave them a heart to know Him. It is no different today, as we turn our heart toward the Lord, we will fall more in love with Him than ever before. In doing so, He will show us more of Himself in the process. I was asked if I would write a poem on the theme for Women's Ministries this year which is A Heart to Know Him. This request inspired this poem.

Think of when you first fell in love. You thought you knew that person well. As time passed you found you had only scratched the surface of that love. It is the same with our relationship with Christ. The more time we spend with Him, the more we find out about Him and the more we love Him.

We also realize that His love is limitless, knows no boundaries. How blessed we are! Whisper Jesus today as you move closer to Him.

A Heart To Know Me

Jeremiah 24:7
I will give them a heart to know me,
that I am the LORD. They will be my people,
and I will be their God,
for they will return to me
with all their heart.

Whisper Jesus

....

When rescued from the enemy
My heart has cause to rejoice
A new freedom and love possess my soul
As I realize that I am His choice

He heard my cry for deliverance
As He saw my sad estate
He turned me from my sinful path
My crooked ways – He made straight

God gives me a heart to know Him
As I turn from me, myself and I
And I focus on Him and His great love
Drawing near as He draws nigh

But really, He has been there all the while
Waiting for me to turn to Him
He made provision for my escape
Before I knew I was lost in sin

Troubles and trials often get my attention
As I skip merrily on my way
It's when I fall into a deep dark hole
I have to look up for the light of day

Then I see His face as He reaches down
Grasping His hand with all my might
I cry to Him for deliverance

Whisper Jesus

And He restores my blind eyes to sight

How could I be so blind and selfish
To ignore His great love for me
When His mercy and grace covers my sin
Causing me to rejoice that I've been set free

For He will give us a heart to know Him
As we turn to Him and Him only
He fills all the void places in our lives
And with Him we are no longer lonely

Thank you Lord for changing our heart
As we draw closer – we love You more
You grow more precious every hour
Our love grows – it's You we truly adore

Tenderize our heart and our spirit
As we walk each day with You
Draw us close and whisper Your love
As we fall deeper in love with You.

Make it so Lord Jesus!

Rebecca A. Keefe
June 21, 2014

A Little Child Sings Sweetly

I was teaching a group of women in Wilbraham one summer several years ago. The lesson was on being a light for Jesus. As part of the lesson I gave each lady a long white taper candle with this saying on it: "Jesus has come to dispel the darkness in your life. Will you light this candle in your home to show that He is Lord?" I have repeated this exercise several times throughout the years. Francis and I call it our "Jesus Candle" – the long white taper candle is set in a pretty candle holder and placed on our kitchen table. It is a solid visual reminder that when that candle is lit, we will try harder to show the love of Jesus. I gave these candles to the Bethany ladies last year and had them turn to each other as they gave each other a candle and repeat this verse and wait for the reply, "Yes I will." So I ask it again – visualize in your mind that I have just passed a lovely white taper candle to you. Now I am asking you this question. "Jesus has come to dispel the darkness in your life. Will you light this candle in your home to show that He is Lord?" What is your answer? Will you say "Yes I will!" I hope so. And in the meantime, also, quietly Whisper Jesus. For it is because of Him that we have a light to shine!

A Little Child Sings Sweetly

A little child sings sweetly
"This little light of mine"
We can light a candle as well
And let our little light shine

Who is your Lord?

Whisper Jesus

Why let our light shine bright?
Who rose from the dead
And put the darkness to flight?

Is He Lord of your life as you
Live out each day?
Does He rule in your heart
Even as you pray?

Jesus dispels the darkness
He meets all your need
Will you light this candle in your home
To show He is Lord indeed?

Rebecca A. Keefe
April 3, 2012

A Prayer – Losing a Loved One

It is never easy to say a final goodbye to a loved one. We, as believers, are assured that it is not a final goodbye. Yet we mourn for the loss we feel and the void that is left as they leave us behind. In a period of grieving it is easy to focus only on our loss until we change our focus and begin to remember the good things. It's a choice really. We can continue to mourn, and a time of grieving is good and necessary. But to continue in the grieving state without ever seeing the light of day, can be damaging to our mental and physical health. May you know the sweet comfort of God as He walks you through this process of losing someone you love dearly - hour by hour - day by day - month by month - year by year. This poem was written when a friend of mine lost her dad. Here again, as we mourn, perhaps the only thing we can say in our grief is the Name of Jesus. "Jesus" "Jesus." All that is needed is to simply whisper His precious name. As we whisper His sweet Name, He hears us and draws near to us too. And if we allow Him to, He will comfort us with His comfort.

Romans 8:38,39 (NLT)

38.For I am convinced that nothing can ever separate us from his love. Death can't, and life can't. The angels can't, and the demons can't. Our fears for today, our worries about tomorrow, and even the powers of hell can't keep God's love away.
Whether we are high above the sky or in the deepest ocean, nothing in all creation will ever be able to separate us from the love of God that is revealed in Christ Jesus our Lord.

What a wonderful hope we have in our Lord!

Whisper Jesus

A Prayer – Losing a Loved One

To say Goodbye always seems so final
Although we knew this day would come
Yet God promises He'll walk beside us
As our loved one enters their heavenly home

Lord, help us focus on the memories
Letting the good outweigh the bad
As we remember the past laughter
Drowning out the times we are sad

There is Hope in the loved one's passing
Heaven is where they now abide
No pain, sorrow or suffering
Ministering angels are by their side

We thank you God for Your comfort
How You heal our broken hearts
We thank You for Your strength
That from us, You never depart

You promised You'd never forsake us
That You would never leave us alone
We thank You we've been forgiven
And by Your blood, sins atoned

Thank You that You take our grief
Whispering comfort from Your Word
You take our tears and sorrow

Whisper Jesus

Letting us know our prayers are heard

And if You say we'll see them again
We rejoice for we know it's true
This life on earth is not all there is
For we have a sweet Hope in You.

You take our grief and sorrow
Though we don't understand Your ways
We rest our hearts in Your sweet hands
Trusting You, as You number our days

Help us cherish the memories that we have
Focusing on the good and not the sad
For You make all things work together
Knowing in time our hearts will be glad

Rebecca A. Keefe
November 2013

Battles

The Israelites would turn from God and then fall into trouble. When they could no longer stand their oppression they would call out to God. In His compassion He rescued them by miraculous means showing them once again that His ways were beyond their comprehension. It is no different today. We may not be fighting the Philistines or armies that were set against Israel, but we are fighting a spiritual battle daily. Ephesians 6 tells us plainly that we are to put on the whole armor of God. And if He equips us, then the battle is won as we march forward in His strength and His power, not our own. Thank you Lord! Here again, we go into battle in His Name. We win the Battle in His Name. But none of this is done without first coming to Him in a quiet place and whispering "Jesus." Sometimes the battle is so bad that it takes our breath away and all we can do is whisper His name. It is then that He hears our prayer and our hearts cry and shows us that He is still in charge. He will work it out for His glory and our good.

Isaiah 54:7 (NLT)

For a brief moment I abandoned you, but with deep compassion I will bring you back.

Ephesians 6:11, 12 (NLT)

Put on the full armor of God so that you can take your stand again the devil's schemes.
For our struggle is not against flesh and blood, but against the rulers, against the authorities against the powers of this dark world and against the spiritual forces of evil in the heavenly realms.

Whisper Jesus

Battles

We look at the battles in scripture
Against overwhelming odds and schemes
Your Word gives such clear examples of
Those forging mountains, valleys and streams

They bowed their knees in Your presence
Hailing you as LORD and King
You showed them Your ways were not their ways
As they fought You gave them songs to sing

Can we fight a battle and be filled with praise
Can we march forward in You each day
Can we listen to hear Your still small voice
Can we bring the fight to You as we pray

The answer is a resounding Yes
You ponder our ways day and night
You lead us in paths only known to You
You endue us with Your power and might

Your Spirit tugs at our heartstrings
You open our ears to hear to Your voice
You show us we'll win the battle
As we make God Almighty our choice

You plan such good things for Your children
Peace in the midst of the storm
You have a plan for the enemy too
No weapon against us will form

Whisper Jesus

Help us step out in faith to meet You
On the battlefield of life that we face
Help us lay ourselves at the foot of the Cross
Where You show us mercy, love and grace

Help us yield up our strength and weakness
To You and You alone
Giving You every situation and circumstance
As we lay ourselves at Your throne

Equipping us with the Full Armor of God
Is what You do at our lowest point
You are on the battlefield with us
Fighting with You will not disappoint

We may not like the battlefield or
The weapons formed against us at all
But You never will forsake or leave us
As on Your Divine Name we call

So by Your strength we'll be faithful
And by Your Spirit we'll stand strong
And by Your wisdom You'll guide us
Because it's to You that we belong!

Thank You Lord Jesus
Make it so in the battlefield today.

Rebecca A. Keefe
October 8, 2013

20

Before – But Now

Before we come to Christ we may live a life of fear in many areas. Some believe that God could never love them in particular. Perhaps God loves everyone else but not them. There is a song that uses the phrase "looking for love in all the wrong places" and that pretty much describes what we do before we find that Christ is the giver of supreme love. He is the one who gives a purpose to our lives. As we began studying about Gideon we saw that he was hiding in fear from his enemies - threshing wheat in a winepress, hidden away so he couldn't be seen. Yet, the wonderful thing about this story is that God saw his sorry estate and came and ministered to him in spite of himself or his enemies, before and after. What a change, and it's because of the presence of the Most High. So it is with us. We are never the same after an encounter with the Most High God. We can try and hide from our enemies and hide from God. Somehow it does no good. God can and will help us overcome the enemy of our soul and He can fight the battle for us using ways we never dreamed. We may think that God does not care. But He does! And God sees us not as failures, but perhaps like Gideon, a 'mighty hero'. God sees our potential long before we come to the understanding that in His sight we have value and He has a plan for each one of us. He saw Gideon who was the least in his tribe, and his tribe the least of the tribes of Israel as well. He showed Gideon a different view of himself. He was not a loser. He was a hero. Believe today that God has a plan for you, just as he told Jeremiah in a much quoted scripture. Jeremiah 29:11 (NLT) "For I know the plans I have for you," says the LORD, "They are plans for good and not for disaster, to give you a future and a hope."

Judges 6:12 (NLT)

The angel of the LORD appeared to him and said, "Mighty hero, the LORD is with you!"

Before – But Now

Before the Angel spoke to Gideon
He was hiding away in fear
But when the Angel's words came forth
They were concise and very clear

As he questioned the Angel's message
He saw God was still on the throne
That God had not forsaken him
But still called him His very own

Discouraged, beaten and forsaken
Is how he pictured his plight
Yet God pictured Gideon in a different role
As He taught him how to fight

The battle begins at home for this warrior
To rid his family of false gods
He had to set the example
Destroy this lie against all odds

And that's what God asks us also to do

Whisper Jesus

Begin now right now here at home
Tear down those things that draw us away
And realize we are not alone

Before we take Jesus as our King
Our own way seems always the best
But now that He's forgiven all our sin
He helps us through each and every test

It's so hard to fight strong enemies
Who want to take away our faith
Yet God shows us He has a strategy
He'll give the victory and keep us safe

Where is the battle I'm supposed to fight
And where does it need to begin
It starts right here in my own dark heart
When I ask Him to forgive my sin

And then I can reach out to others
To share the Good News so sweet
I can show the love of Jesus
At home and on the street

I can face my fears like Gideon
Receive answers and hear God's plan
He'll strengthen me for the battle to come
He'll show me how and where to stand

Before, I may have been fearful
Looking inward instead of to Him

Whisper Jesus

But now I can be like Gideon
Fight the enemy and purpose to win

Make it so Lord Jesus!

Rebecca A. Keefe
September 24, 2013

<u>Button Your Lip</u>

My husband Francis and I often joke with one another when having a heated discussion. When you place an Irishman and an Italian lady together, there are bound to be differences. Often the discussion will end when he says: "Go ahead! Have the last word." Sometimes I do and other times I don't. But, I've got to tell you, that is hard! Also, growing up with an Italian Mama, we were never allowed to say those dreaded words "Shut Up!" It just wasn't allowed or tolerated. She would say to us "Be quiet" or "Hush" or "Button Your Lip" – or "Shush" but never "Shut Up." Although my Nonno would come close when he would say in his broken Italian "Shutt-um Up-pa you Face-a." It is difficult when we want to have the last word, but most times, like this poem, we just need to "Button our Lip." Button Your Lip is also a reminder of how much our mouth can get us into trouble or we can pray! My Mama was the one in our family who encouraged me to pray about anything and everything day or night. Just be quiet and pray about it. Those were words spoken to me when I was a teenager. I can still hear them speaking to me today. "Button you lip Becky and pray about it." The scripture is pretty clear also on keeping quiet, another time to button my lip and simply whisper "Jesus."

Proverbs 15:1 (NLT)

A gentle answer turns away wrath, but harsh words stir up anger.
The wise person makes learning a joy; fools spout only foolishness.

Psalm 46:10 (NLT)

Be silent, and know that I am God!

Button Your Lip

"Be still and listen." My Mama would say.
"Button your lip and learn to pray."
"But Mama, can God hear me when I cry?"
"Yes, child." she'd answer. "He can even hear your sigh."

"It's hard to be quiet and button my lip
I know the way and it's quite a trip.
I have to tell Jesus just what to do
I know my problem much better than you!"

And then I look at my half-baked plan
Seeing God's view is a much broader span.
Then hear again His sweet wisdom anew,
With Mama's words ringing sweet and true.

"Be still and listen." My Mama would say
"Button your lip and learn to pray.
You'll see God move in marvelous ways
As you Button Your lip and learn to pray."

Rebecca A. Keefe
June 6, 2011

Cold Dark Place

O Mighty Man of Valor! Wait! What?! Me?! Unbelievable! Not me! Have you taken a good look at me?! Yet, God sees in us something we cannot see in ourselves. He looks beyond our frail humanity and sees what we can become in Him. What a marvelous God we serve. He takes us from the ordinary and shows us what He can do – that His plan and His ways are so much different than what we would try to do. How many times have you and I tried to accomplish something and it kept failing? Then, when we are about to give up, we turn in desperation to God and He then shows us His way. My reaction so many times is something like: "Oh! I get it now! You can accomplish all things for Your purpose! You just want me to get out of the way!" It's a lesson I seem to learn over and over. This stubborn, determined nature of mine keeps wanting to do it my way! God not only works in us – He works through us if we allow Him to. What about you? Are you struggling? Have you thought about giving your struggle to Jesus and letting Him do the work? It's so much easier that way. If you feel you are in a cold dark place, why not find a quiet place alone and simply whisper the sweet and precious Name of Jesus. No noise of the telephone, radio, computer, social media, just a quiet place. Allow yourself to breathe. And then simply whisper "Jesus."

Cold Dark Place

Judges/Chapters 6-7-8

Gideon worked in a cold dark place
Threshing wheat in a wine press no less
He was isolated and full of fear
And his nation was in distress

Under an Oak tree, hidden from view
The Angel of God drew near
It was evident God could see him
Even though he was riddled with fear

Yet he was faithful to do his task
When he was hidden from sun and wind
He kept praying for a deliverer
Wondering who his God would send

"Behold O Valiant Warrior!"
The Angel called as he drew in close
Gideon was alone in his cold dark place
His hiding place was exposed

"You are the one I have chosen
To defeat the enemies at hand"
Gideon wondered how this could happen
How could God save this beleaguered land

Yet God showed He does things different
He chooses those whom He will
He comes to the cold dark place in our lives
And increases our gifts and our skill

Whisper Jesus

Staying hidden from sight and beaten
Is where our enemy would have us be
But Jesus has come to break those bonds
And to set His people free

He shows us in hard and trying times
He has not forgotten our name
Our cries have been heard in heaven above
With Him things are not the same

Our crisis will never take us
Where God cannot hear our cry
He will show Himself in our cold dark place
And will dry the tears from our eyes

He'll equip us for the battle
When we feel beaten and alone
And He'll move in ways we cannot dream
As we stop doing things on our own

His ways are so much higher than ours
His Word is trusted and true
As we place our future in His hands
He says "Trust me I'll work through you"

Help us Lord to be Valiant Warriors
Yielding to Your will each day
Help us trust you fully without question
As You direct us on our way

Make it so Lord Jesus

Rebecca A. Keefe
September 17, 2013

Disappointment vs. His Appointment

One Sunday morning not long ago, our pastor gave a message on Disappointment vs. His Appointment and stressed the fact that three little letters could make a tremendous difference in a word. Add-Dis-to the word Appointment and it changes its meaning completely. As I was "thoughting" I was reminded of the truth of this. We seem to remember the disappointments so much more than the appointments. Yet, I sincerely believe there are divine appointments for each one of us. God ordained happenings that occur in our everyday lives that bring meaning and fulfillment in a moment's notice. We need to be alert and aware that our God is working all the time on our behalf so that His name may be glorified. We also need to be aware that the enemy of our soul is equally intent on destroying those divine appointments or cause us to miss them.

"O God, keep us alert and aware! Again, Lord, it's all I can do sometimes when disappointment comes my way, to just whisper Your name "Jesus." Sometimes it seems I have had the breath knocked out of me by some unexpected circumstance. Yet if I can just quiet myself and focus on You, I know You will whisper my name too. Your Word says, "They that wait upon You will renew their strength." Disappointments can sap strength completely away; leaving me sucked dry. Sweet Jesus, hear our hearts cry."

After "thoughting" about these two words this poem was born.

Isaiah 40:31 (KJV)

But they that wait upon the Lord shall renew their strength; they shall mount up with wings as eagles; they shall run and not be weary; and they shall walk and not faint.

Disappointment vs His Appointment

One little letter from D to H
Changes things that I view
Sad and disappointed
Til I see His point of view

Disappointed over the things
I've planned so carefully
His Appointments show what happens
When I do things prayerfully

Waiting for the test to pass
Makes me impatient, at the best
His Appointments always show
That the wait is worth the test

Waiting on the Lord I know
Renews my strength somehow
But I want – what I want – when I want it
And I always want it now

Whisper Jesus

So help me Lord to wait on You
Slow down and wait to hear
Cause disappointments to fade away
Calm my heart as I draw near

Your appointments are always best
Your ways so much better than mine
Help me Lord to hear Your voice
Heed Your Appointments Divine.

Your Word gives clear direction
By Your grace I'll listen more
Renew my strength as I wait for You
As I reap what You have in store.

I want what I want – and I want it now
But I want what You want too
Help me win the battle over myself
As I learn to wait on You.

Make it so, Lord Jesus
Amen

Rebecca A. Keefe
May 28, 2013

Does God Ever Make Mistakes

We have been studying about the attributes of God and asking the following questions: Does God Care? Does He really hear us when we pray? Is God fair? In line with those questions this poem was born. We tend to box God in and think that He can only move within parameters that we understand. Yet, He constantly shows us that, just as it says in His Word, His ways are so much higher than ours and His thoughts are so much higher than ours. His plans for us go far beyond what we could imagine. We just need to climb out of the box ourselves and lean hard onto our sweet Lord and let our faith grow as we trust God to work things out, letting go of wanting our way all the time and learning that His way is always best. He truly does not make mistakes. As we move in close enough to Whisper His Name "Jesus" we will hear His whisper back to us. He gives us the confidence to trust Him wholly and to trust that He does all things well.

Deuteronomy 32:4 (NIV)

He is the Rock, his works are perfect, and all his ways are just. A faithful God who does no wrong, upright and just is he.

2 Samuel 22:31 (NIV)

As for God, his way is perfect; The Lord's way is flawless; he shields all who take refuge in him.

Psalm 18:30 (NIV)

As for God, his way is perfect: The Lord's word is flawless; he shields all who take refuge in him.

Does God Ever Make Mistakes

As we go through life as it happens
With joy as well as sorrow
I find myself wondering at the way God works
As I face each day and each tomorrow

There are things that I would love to have
Prayers prayed with sincere devotion
Yet sometimes God answers with a "No"
And I'm left with life in slow motion

That life would be easy without grief or distress
That's my wish for me and you each day
That there would be no trouble or woe
Peace and happiness would be here to stay

But then I would be living a fairy tale
With kings and princes and queens
Where we all live happily ever after
Accomplishing happiness by any means

Whisper Jesus

God shows us always in His Word
That His ways are past finding out
That He has a plan and a purpose for us
Even though we stumble and sometimes doubt

Is God fair, does He hear my prayer
Is He there, and does He ever make a mistake?
I don't need to be judge and jury of my life
I need to trust that He knows what's at stake

Do I ever complain and whine a bit
If God's sees a different way than mine
The answer is "yes" I can be a whiner
But I can always trust His design

His Word declares God is perfect
His perspective and outreach is greater
If He can form me from the dust of the earth
Then surely I can trust my Creator

Lord, I don't claim to understand it all
But I do know Your word will never fail
You promise to walk each step with me
And that Your love will always prevail

The devil would have us doubt and complain
Asking if God cares about our lives
When this happens we must go to His Word
Where it states the devil is the master of lies

Help us remember sweet Savior and Friend

Whisper Jesus

That Your love and mercy covers our sin
You walk with us and talk with us
And place Your sweet Peace within

We trust in Your mercy and grace
We make mistakes but not You!
We love you dear Lord Jesus,
We Thank you for Your love too.

Rebecca A. Keefe
June 17, 2014

Enduring Faith

There are so many things we take by 'faith' or take for granted in life as this poem talks about. It is not until something rocks our world that we begin to look around with different eyes. For instance, we go through a hurtful time and as a result we look at those around us with a different perspective because of where we have recently been. Many times at a funeral folks are not so much looking for us to give them an answer as to why their loved one died. They are just looking for us to be there. All we need to say is we are sorry for their loss. I worked in a funeral home for several years when I was a young pastor's wife. I saw firsthand how meaningful it was when people show up to hug the grieving person. No one is looking for answers at that time. The important thing is that we go to that uncomfortable place - just be there. Be self-conscious if you must, stand on one foot and then the other, be nervous and just be there. How does our faith endure during hard times? It endures because we have people around us who are there as if they were ministering to Christ Himself. In truth we would rather be at a picnic, not at a place of grief. In reality, the grieving one may want to be at a picnic too instead of standing beside the casket. Christ asks us to get out of our comfort zone, go to that uncomfortable place of ministry and be the arms of Christ and share His love. After the commotion, show up in person and spend time together. Just be there with your enduring faith and show the hurting person that Jesus is the author of enduring faith. Perhaps as you walk into that grieving person's home you may be quietly whispering the sweet and powerful Name of Jesus. Ask Jesus to simply let you be an extension of Him to bless and build up others. "Sweet Jesus - I don't know what to say or what to do, so I ask that You allow me to be Your arms extended to my hurting friend." Just simply and humbly and quietly Whisper Jesus.

Colossian 3:17 (NLT)

Whatever you do in word or deed, do all in the name of the Lord Jesus, giving thanks through Him to God the Father.

Enduring Faith

So many things we take by faith
As we travel on this way
The flowers that grow, the rain that falls
And the sun that brightens our day

The air we breathe, the food we eat
The bed we sleep in at night
The house where we live, the roads that we walk
And the lights that shine so bright

What if a storm blew it all away
And all we knew was gone
Could we still come to God with our faith in tact
Could we still be singing a song?

We watch the news, but it's not us
And we forget there are those in need
Help us Lord to be mindful still

Of our brothers and sisters indeed.

How can we help, what can we do
As we live our lives day by day
Help us sweet Lord to remember them
Above all else – we can be there and we CAN pray.

If there is a way that we can meet the need
If there is something we can do
Please show us just what in our quiet way
We can help and bring Glory to you.

Let us not forget there are those in despair
Who need Your help and care
Use us as Your arms extended
Show us whose burden to share.

We've nothing to give – our monies are few
Where do we go and what shall we do?
The need is great but You're greater still
Help us dear Lord, to seek Your will.

It's not just money to meet the need
It's a hug, or a call or freshly baked bread
A gentle touch, a thoughtful deed
It's a dinner date with the table spread.

If we can spent time with a friend in grief
Who has lost a loved one dear
It's as if we're doing it for you Dear Lord
As we help wipe away their tear

Whisper Jesus

Rebecca A. Keefe
May 15, 2011

<u>Fixing My Eyes Upon Jesus</u>

What has grabbed your attention today, something bright and shiny? Was it a person, place or thing that you "fixed" your eyes and attention on? Today there is so much out there to grab our attention. I find it a challenge to refrain from booting up my computer in the morning and checking out Facebook or email before I begin to do anything else. Yet, when I can get my cup of coffee, sit at my kitchen table, open the Bible, and devotional book and journal I find my day goes so much smoother. But sometimes, I confess, I get sidetracked. My eyes see the dishes from last night's snack and I think "I'll just put these in the dishwasher before I sit down." Then I discover the dishwasher if full and needs to be emptied. So I empty that and then load the snack dishes. I remember I need to do a load of white things, and it should only take a minute to throw those in the washing machine. So I trot downstairs and start the wash. While I'm there I may as well fold the clothes in the dryer so it will be empty for the wash. Before I know it – my eyes have been drawn to everything else except what I had intended to do first thing in the morning! Time has a way of doing that to us doesn't it? So let this poem encourage you to "Fix Your Eyes on Jesus" and just sit at your kitchen table quietly, and perhaps start out by just whispering the sweet and powerful name of Jesus.

Hebrews 3:1 (NIV)

Therefore, holy brothers, who share in the heavenly calling, fix your thoughts on Jesus, the apostle and high priest whom we confess.

Hebrews 12:1 & 2 (NIV)

Let us fix our eyes on Jesus, the author and perfecter of our faith, who for the joy set before him endured the cross, scorning its shame and sat down at the right hand of the throne of God.

Revelation 22:17 (NIV)

The Spirit and the bride say, "Come!" And let him who hears say "Come!" Whoever is thirsty, let him come; and whoever wishes, let him take the free gift of the water of life.

Fixing My Eyes upon Jesus

If I fix my eyes on Jesus
Instead of fixing things on my own
I might not have made such a mess of things
If I'd have placed my need at His Throne

Sometime I rush headlong into my life
Thinking of all the best solutions
I think of all the ends and outs
Coming to my own conclusions

Life is hard with its ups and downs
It's a hard race we are called to run
Yet He promised rest for the weary
And in the end His words: "Well Done"

It's so easy to forget where we're headed
In this road called "Life" everyday

Whisper Jesus

We get sidetracked by comments of people
Worrying what they will have to say

Yet God promises His grace is sufficient
For every trial and every need
He gives grace and mercy as we travel
Assuring us – in Him – we'll succeed

He didn't promise an easy road
As His children we called to press on
To finish the race he's set before us
Running with faith until the victory is won

We all will receive a victor's crown
As we keep our eyes on the goal
Not looking back to see who's behind
Trusting Him to keep us upright and whole

So we look with great anticipation and joy
Knowing He bids us run on, don't stop, but come
Finish the race though tired and worn
He'll be there to welcome us Home

Sweet Jesus help us always remember
You are never far from our side
You've planned this race we are running
You are our Help and our unfailing guide

Thank You sweet Lord for your promise
Thank You that Your Word is true
Thank You for our Home in Heaven

Thank you that You'll Bring us Through!

Rebecca A. Keefe
April 22, 2014
Free Indeed

When the Bible states that God forgives our iniquities and our sins, that He will remember them no more, it thrills me! There are times we remember all the wrongs that have been committed against us personally. It is with great effort that we try to forget. Our minds are like computers, storing a tremendous amount of information both good and bad. Just when we think we may have forgiven someone or something, an old offense can suddenly pop into our minds. It is then with great effort that we choose to forget. The same thing happens when we remember offenses and sins we may have committed against God. It is then our Lord and Savior can say to us: "What offense? What sin, I don't remember." That's what redemption and salvation are all about. We are free indeed. We could shout our gratitude or we could simply Whisper "Jesus." "Thank You."

Jeremiah 31:34 (NIV)

For I will forgive their wickedness and will remember their sins no more.

Psalm 103:8-12 (NLT)

The LORD is merciful and gracious; he is slow to get angry and full of unfailing love.
He will not constantly accuse, nor remain angry forever.

He has not punished us for all our sins, nor does he deal with us as
we deserve.
For his unfailing love toward those who fear him is as great as the
height of the heavens above the earth.
He has removed our rebellious acts as far away from us as the east is
from the west.

John 8:36 (NIV)

So if the Son makes you free, you will be free indeed.

Free Indeed

How blessed we are that God loves us
And made a way of escape from our sin
We are no longer condemned or lost
When we ask Christ to dwell within

Covenants from Abraham to David
New covenant through Christ our Lord
To those who were in the Upper Room
All gathered in one accord

To us right here in this present day
Forgiveness of sin is free
All we need to do is ask
Sweet Jesus – Please forgive me!

Salvation so rich and sweet
The Holy Spirit to infill our being
The New Covenant in Christ is ours

Whisper Jesus

No longer blind but now, seeing

Perhaps you've never known Him
Who takes all guilt and sin away
Let me introduce you to Jesus
Who wants to come into your heart to stay

Forgiveness of sin and despair
From guilt and sorrow set free
"If the Son sets you free
you are free indeed"

Ask Jesus to come into your heart
You will experience joy beyond measure
You'll find a new freedom from your guilt
And experience a Love you will treasure

Covenants old and new in Christ
Promises of God – forever
His love is lasting, sure and solid
And He will leave me – never!

Thank You Sweet Lord
That You died for me!

Rebecca A. Keefe
February 25, 2014

Forgiveness

The entire Psalm 139 is so beautiful and shows the power of our all-seeing God, who is all-powerful, and is everywhere present. How wonderful is that? Try as we may, we can never hide from our precious Lord. It is a scary but wonderful phenomenon to me. The God I love and serve is aware of me in this vast endless universe. He knows me by name. He is aware of me! At the same time, if I am up to mischief He knows that too! So it is sobering and awesome at the same time. Yet, in the midst of it all, His forgiveness is there for me and you as we confess our sins. And because of His forgiveness we can in turn forgive others. Is it easy? Not by a long shot! But it becomes easier as we give it over to Jesus and let Him handle it. After all, He is the Master Forgiver! And because He is the Master Forgiver I have the privilege to sit quietly in His presence and simply whisper "Jesus." "Have mercy on me."

Psalm 139:1,2 & 9-11 (NLT)

LORD, you have examined my heart and know everything about me.
You know when I sit down or stand up.
You know my every thought when far away.
If I ride the wings of the morning, if I dwell by the farthest oceans,
even there your hand will guide me, and your strength will support me.
I could ask the darkness to hide me and the light around me to become night – but even in darkness I cannot hide from you.

Forgiveness

I remember – "I've Got a Secret"
The name of an old game show
We had to guess just what it was
So that the whole world could know

Yet when a secret is not a game
And the stakes are higher than life
We try to hide the truth from others
And it brings us all kinds of strife

This is the reason our Savior has come
To reveal the secrets of God
He sees our lives in their messed up state
As He ponders the paths we've trod

He's taken my bad secrets
Cleansed my heart and paid my due
He's placed his secret love in my heart
And made me, in Him, brand new

Forgiven, covered and not counted
That's what happens when I repent
He covers my sins with His precious blood
At the cross with no more torment

The good secret I now hold in my heart
Is His Love and His Mercy so true
He reached down and erased my bad secrets
And has made my life brand new.

Whisper Jesus

His unfailing love surrounds me
As I trust and believe on Him
He guides me and watches over me
Takes away my sorrow and dwells within

So I can rejoice like His Word tells me
I can be glad as I obey his commands
I can shout for Joy for sins forgiven
As I place my life in His hands

Thank You Lord Jesus!

Rebecca A. Keefe
November 5, 2013

Fragrance vs. Stench

There is beautiful story of Mary in the Gospels where she anoints Jesus with a costly bottle of perfume much to the chagrin of Judas and wonderment of the disciples. Jesus says her act of devotion will be talked about for centuries to come – and it has been and still is. She caught a glimpse of what Jesus was talking about – perhaps she understood that he was going to die – but I doubt anyone really grasped what was about to happen.

------and the fragrance filled the house------

What I want to focus on in this particular story is the aroma of that perfume. How it must have filled that room with a strong aroma. Not a stink, or a smell, but a wonderful rich aroma. It must have lingered for days or weeks afterward. Do you have a favorite aroma or smell that triggers a memory of something pleasant? I do. When I catch a hint of some Italian spices it brings me right back to my Italian Nonna's kitchen or my Nonno's wine cellar. Pleasant aromas, good memories, warm feelings.

In Mary's time long after that incident and Jesus' death, and resurrection – whenever they would catch a whiff of that perfume, they would be transported back to that moment in time…. And they would remember the words of Jesus –

The question to ask ourselves is:
"What kind of aroma do we leave behind?"
Is it pleasant or is it more like a stink or stench?

Whisper Jesus

The easiest way to turn a stench into a fragrance is to find a quiet place where we can simply whisper the sweet and powerful Name of Jesus. We can ask that He forgive our sins, and He will. He cleans away the bad stench of sin and clothes us in His righteousness and beauty. And through Him we begin to embody His fragrance. Simply whisper Jesus and invite Him into your life today. You will be glad you did. God Bless you!

John12:1-7 (NLT)

1 Six days before the Passover celebration began, Jesus arrived in Bethany, the home of Lazarus—the man he had raised from the dead.

2 A dinner was prepared in Jesus' honor. Martha served, and Lazarus was among those who ate with him.

3 Then Mary took a twelve-ounce of expensive perfume made from essence of nard, and she anointed Jesus' feet with it, wiping his feet with her hair. The house was filled with the fragrance.

4 But Judas Iscariot, the disciple who would soon betray him, said,

5 "That perfume was worth a year's wages. It should have been sold and the money given to the poor."

6 Not that he cared for the poor—he was a thief, and since he was in charge of the disciples' money, he often stole some for himself.

7 Jesus replied, "Leave her alone. She did this in preparation for my burial."

Whisper Jesus

Fragrance versus Stench

There is a story in the Bible
About expensive perfume in a jar
That was poured over the feet of Jesus
While witnesses thought it bizarre

The people gasped as they saw it happen
As Mary began to weep
They thought it way too expensive
To be wasted on somebody's feet

Then Jesus began to tell them
As the fragrance filled the room
That what she had done was a sacrifice
Preparing for His burial in a tomb

They didn't understand His words
For they thought He was there to stay
To raise the dead and heal the sick
And forgive them for going astray

Long after this incident happened
As people would pass this place
They caught a whiff of this fragrance
And remembered His tender embrace

Is my love for Jesus like Mary's
Leaving a sweet fragrance behind
Do I cause a stench or odor

Whisper Jesus

By words and actions unkind

Lord, I want to be a fragrance
Where the aroma is rich and pure
I want my actions to speak louder than words
Showing You are the Divine cure

Help not to leave a stench in my wake
But an odor that brings glory to You
Let my testimony of Your love
All ring pleasant and true

A fragrance or a stench
That's the question we ask today
With Your help Lord, we'll be an aroma
Others will remember long after today

Make it so Lord Jesus!

Rebecca A. Keefe
August 1, 2014

Get Rid of The Baggage!

So many times we think a brand new year will start out wonderfully new, when we have to realize our journey is still in progress. Like any journey we pack our bags for the trip. Sometimes we put everything but the kitchens sink in our suitcases, and then as we travel we pare down. So it is in our lives. We realize the things we carry around with us are not the things we necessarily need. There are some things we need to get rid of completely along the way and just leave by the wayside. Better yet, just give to Jesus entirely. Can you stop right now; lift your baggage up to our sweet Lord? Then simply whisper "Jesus." As you begin to understand that He loves you and wants to carry that nasty baggage you will experience a new found freedom. The only thing He needs from us is a willing heart to hand it over to Him. Go ahead. Lift it up to Him right now. You'll be glad you did!

Psalm 68:19 (NIV)
Praise be to the Lord, to God our Savior, who daily bears our burdens.

Get Rid of The Baggage!

I have to Hang On
So says that old adage
I need to solve my dilemma
While hanging on to the baggage

Let Go and Let God
Can I do that just now?
Let Him take the problem

Whisper Jesus

And not telling Him how?

Lord, You surely need me
To be fully in charge
Why, I can handle anything
Small, medium or large!

I know I get so tired
Of holding on so tight
I'm using all my strength
And using all my might!

Your plan is better
My heart knows it's true
But my grip is so tight
It's hard to give it to You

Try me and see
You say loud and clear
Okay – I'll let go
I give you my gear

I've held on for so long
It might take some time
So – you solve the dilemma
It's Yours and not mine

Getting rid of the baggage
I'll carry it no longer
Now You hold that bag
As You make me stronger

Amen
Rebecca A. Keefe
September 18, 2012

God Do You Care?

Have you ever asked that question, "God, Can You hear me?" God, can you see me? God, do You Care? There have been times in my life when I wondered if God may have forgotten my name! When my marriage fell apart and I stood in a court room hearing the judge say the marriage was now dissolved. It was like walking through life in a daze. When I lay in the hospital with tubes and IV's stuck everywhere, when my body was wracked with pain and two separate e-coli infections. Those were dark times. Whew! Not just one operation but seven. I knew God cared because He gave me a Peace in my heart that I knew came only from Him. I'm not talking about serenity, I talking about Peace. Even though I was in a dark time of despair and when I seriously physically ill, I still was confident that God was with me. Does God care? Yes He does! Will we go through dark times and trials? Yes we will! Does it mean He no longer cares for us? No way! He moves in ways we cannot understand as these scriptures relate. Even when we can't see Him, He is there and always will be. May God minister to you in unspeakable ways if you are going through a dark time now. He will bring you through. There were many nights in a month long stay in the hospital that all I could do was Whisper the sweet Name of Jesus. Just whispering His name brought me peace. God is no respecter of persons. He can bring peace to your troubled heart as well.

Daniel 3:17-18 & 23-25 (NASB)

If it be so, our God whom we serve is able to deliver us from the furnace of blazing fire; and He will deliver us out your hand, O king. But even if He does not, let it be known to you, O king, We will not worship the golden image that you have set up

But these three men, Shadrach, Meshach and Abed-nego fell into the midst of the furnace of blazing fire still tied up

then Nebuchadnezzar the king was astounded and stood up in haste; he said to his high officials, "Was it not three men we cast bound into the midst of the fire?" They replied to the king, "Certainly, O king."

He said, "Look! I see four men loosed and walking about in the midst of the fire without harm, and the appearance of the fourth is like a son of the gods!"

Luke 10:30-35 (NASB)

Read these verses about the story of the Good Samaritan who stopped to minister to the fallen man after the priest and the Levite passed him by.

Hebrews 13:8 (NASB)

Jesus Christ is the same yesterday and today and forever;

I Peter 5:6-7 (NASB)

Therefore, humble yourselves under the mighty hand of God, that He may exalt you at the proper time.
Casting all your anxiety (care) on Him, because He cares for you.

God, Do You Care?

Whisper Jesus

There are so many stories in the Bible
That talk about God's sweet intervention
Which show us He does things differently
Perhaps just to get our attention

Take the three Hebrew men in the furnace
Who refused to bow down to the king
Who trusted God to deliver them - or - not
They would still His praises sing

Right there in the middle of the heat and fire
The Son of God came and stood close by
No hair on their heads was even singed
Their flesh was cool and calm and dry

Then take the story of the man who was robbed
As he traveled all alone one day
Three people walked right past this man
Even though two knew how to pray

But one man stopped to minister
To the man who was beaten down
The Samaritan reached out and helped him
And took him to a room in town

We often identify with the Samaritan
Who stopped to help the man in need
But what if we were that man in trouble
Would we think Jesus could see us bleed?

He may not answer the way we want

Whisper Jesus

Or even give us what we're asking for
But He asks that we wait for His timing
And when He's ready He may open a door

We are so set on what we want when we want it
And we question "God, Do You Really Care?
Can't you see that I'm in quite a mess
How many times must I come to You in prayer?"

Three Hebrew men when threatened with death
Loving God were determined to stand
They were thrown into a fiery furnace
Where the hottest flames were fanned

Yet God chose an unconventional manner
To rescue these faithful few
And He sent an unlikely person
To minister to the fallen man too

God is the same yesterday, today and forever
He sees our fallen estate
We may think He doesn't care about us
But when He answers – He's never late

So cast your cares upon Jesus
Tell Him all your sorrows and care
He will bring the answer as you trust in Him
As you wait humbly – kneeling in prayer

We know You care Lord Jesus
Give us Your grace to wait and be still

Help us to trust You fully
Relying completely on Your Divine will.

Make it so Lord Jesus

Rebecca A. Keefe
May 13, 2014

God's Fairness

We often hear people blame God when things happen in their lives. Why me? Why now? Why did God let this happen? These are questions that we hear all the time. If something goes wrong it's God's fault and God is not fair. Have you ever said that as a child to your parents? "It's not fair!" And their response might have been "Life's not fair, get over it!" Why is it we are so prone to blame God when things go topsy turvy in our lives? I suppose some of it may be that we want what we want when we want it and we want it right now! I've said that before and it really seems to be the bottom line, me, mine and now. Yet, in the end, we can stop the blame game. Come humbly to our loving God who can and will walk beside us and guide us through whatever storm we are facing. Let me encourage you to come to Him. He can show you that He is loving and compassionate and gracious. Thank you Lord! And again, simply come to Him quietly and just Whisper "Jesus" It will change your perspective completely as you begin to realize He loves you and truly does care for you. You begin to view your circumstance from a different perspective as He opens your understanding. It is worth time spent when you simply and humbly, quietly and reverently Whisper Jesus.

Psalm 103:8-14 & 17 (NIV)

The LORD is compassionate and gracious, Slow to anger and abounding in loving kindness.
He will not always strive with us, nor will He keep His anger forever.
He has not dealt with us according to our sins, nor rewarded us according to our iniquities
For as high as the heavens are above the earth, So great is His loving kindness toward those who fear Him.

As far as the east is from the west, So far has He removed our transgressions from us.

Just as a father has compassion on his children, So the LORD has compassion on those who fear Him.

For He Himself knows our frame; He is mindful that we are but dust.

17 But the loving-kindness of the LORD is from everlasting to everlasting on those who fear Him and His righteousness to children's children.

God's Fairness

In a world filled with selfishness and greed
Where the emphasis is ME and only ME
It sometimes seems so hard to focus
On my sweet Lord who came to set me free

The feeling is "What I deserve right now,
What I am entitled to and all"
Yet in God's economy and plan
It's on His Name I need to call

Should He give me what I deserve?
Then I am doomed beyond all hope and reason
For I'm only a sinner saved by Grace
A Child of God now through every season

To forgive my sin – what a glorious thought
Thrown as far as the East is from the West
I deserve death and punishment

Whisper Jesus

Yet through Him I'm renewed and blessed

His Mercy dictates healing my wounds
Received by the enemies blows
His compassion completely encompasses my soul
As I yield to Him above and below

If the disciples demanded fair treatment
Wanting only a kingdom on earth
Then they'd never been called by Jesus
Knowing their faith would prove their worth

Just look at those whom God has chosen
David, Esther, Matthew, Mark, Luke and John
You and I can name countless others
Who faced death yet – still determined to hang on

Was God fair in all this happening
Were they entitled to live forever too
He could raise Jesus from the dead
If He could not raise them – was God true?

Thank You Lord, – Your ways are not my ways
You still have a plan for my life
You've promised to go before and behind
To be with me in all kinds of strife

All You ask is that I trust You
To work things out for my good
To bring You honor and glory and praise
Even though Your answer may be misunderstood

Whisper Jesus

So I place my trembling heart in Your hands
Trusting You to be Holy and Just
You breathed into me the Breath of Life
Even though my frame is but dust.

Thank You for doing things better
Than I could even ask or dream
Your way of answering all my prayers
Is always best and always supreme.

By Your Grace and Mercy
Let me be numbered among those
Who trust You fully – Make it so Lord Jesus!

Rebecca A. Keefe
May 20, 2014

<u>God's Love</u>

The Bible teaches about how we are made alive in Christ. Paul describes it best in Ephesians 2. The more we read about God's love, the more we see or catch just a glimmer of how deep his love reaches. We are made not only alive but brand new. It is the divine hope that we have. This life here on earth is not all there is! God has so much more through His Son. Have you thought about God's Love lately, because life is not so much about us – but all about Him? We can't explain the love of God, or even try to understand it. I know I can't. But I can accept it and softly Whisper "Thank You Jesus."

Ephesians 2:1-2, 4-5 (NIV)

As for you, you were dead in your transgressions and sins,
in which you used to live when you followed the ways of this world
…..
 But because of His great love for us, God, who is rich in mercy,
made us alive with Christ even when we were dead in transgressions
– it is by grace you have been saved.

God's Love

Great stories of Love
Often go against reason
Showing mercy and grace
In all kinds of seasons

Compassion and forgiveness
That keeps reaching beyond

Whisper Jesus

Limitless – unending
Creating love's strong bond

That's the way God loves me
Beyond my wildest dreams
He casts aside my failings
And all my foolish schemes

He shows me that I'm worthy
That His love will never end
He gives me joy and glory
He's my Forever Friend

I truly don't deserve Him
But He died that I might live
His heart now beats in my heart
His love I'll never outlive

Turning from my faithlessness
Confessing all my sin
Allows His love to flow freely
As I turn my life to Him

Thank You God for Your promise
That your anger is turned away
Thank You for Grace and Mercy
Thank You – Your Love is here to stay.

Thank You Jesus!
Rebecca A. Keefe
June 4, 2013

Grace Upon Grace

Grace Upon Grace. I gladly accept this, but I may never in my humanness fully understand it. Jonathan and David in the Old Testament in I Samuel 18:3-4 made a divine covenant with each other. Jonathan stripped himself of his robe and armor including his sword and belt and bestowed it all on David. Jonathan recognized David as God's anointed one. Their covenant included entrusting each other into the LORD's hands forever. This included their children as well, each vowing to care for the others' families now and in the future. (I Samuel 20:42) This was because of his great love for David and for God. This stands as a reminder and a clear picture of how Christ made an everlasting covenant with us, stripping Himself of His heavenly robe because He loved us. He did this so he could cloth us in His righteousness through His divine grace and mercy. And because of His grace and mercy we are entrusted into God's hands forever, an everlasting covenant. We are so blessed! Grace upon Grace. I don't understand it, but I accept it. "Thank you sweet Jesus that you extend your Grace to the likes of me! This causes me also, to bow in Your presence and simply whisper Jesus. You are so worthy of our praise, thank you Lord for Your great love."

John 1:16 (NASB)
For of His fullness we have all received, and grace upon grace.

John 1:16 (NIV)

We have all benefited from the rich blessings he brought to us – one gracious blessing after another.

I Samuel 18:3–4 (NASB)

Then Jonathan made a covenant with David because he loved him as himself.
Jonathan stripped himself of the robe that he had on him and gave it to David, and his armor, including his sword and his bow and his belt.

Grace Upon Grace

John 1:16
For of His fullness we have all received, and grace upon grace.

Grace upon Grace, what does it mean?
One Gracious blessing after another
Not under the law of Moses
But grace and mercy like no other

Clothed in the likeness of man
Our Lord came to the earth below
He came with healing in His wings
And grace to us to bestow

Grace upon Grace, how can this be
For a sinful one such as I
No limits to God's wonderful grace
When I call He hears my cry

The longer I know Him and love Him

Whisper Jesus

My faith grows stronger still
As I thank Him for His goodness
Asking direction for His will

I may falter in my weakness
But when I come back to Him
His hand of grace extends to me
As He forgives me of my sin

He clothes me with His armor
His robe of righteousness mine to wear
Just like Jonathan gave to David
God's armor is mine to share

So I walk forward into battle
Knowing my armor is fully in place
He gives victory over my enemies
As he gives me Grace upon Grace.

Make it so Lord Jesus!

Rebecca A. Keefe
January 18, 2014

<u>Hanging On or Letting Go</u>

Should I hang on or let go? Especially when I have fought hard to gain ground and then see it slipping precariously out of my hands! Have you ever been blown out of the water with a situation that caught you by surprise? I have! Whenever that happens, after the shock, and after trying to fix it myself, I finally give it to God. But I have to be honest here; I am so guilty of trying to hang on trying to fix things longer than I should. It's so hard for me to let go. But, usually, after I struggle and fuss and fume, I give up in exasperation to God. It is then, when I say "I give up" that God's peace floods my spirit and I wonder why I didn't turn things over to Him in the first place. I need to ask God for wisdom for every situation of whether to hang on or let it go. The Apostle Paul admonishes us to bring everything to God! The difficult part is the decision of what to do. So what are you hanging on to right now? What do you need to let go? Why not do some "thoughting" on that subject for a while. And why not just simply Whisper Jesus right now, and hand over what you are struggling with. You'll be glad you did.

Philippians 4:6-7 (NIV)

Do not be anxious about anything, but in everything by prayer and petition, with thanksgiving present your requests to God.

And the peace of God, which transcends all understanding, will guard your hearts and your minds in Christ Jesus.

Hanging On or Letting Go

Hanging on or letting go

Whisper Jesus

Palms up or fists tight
Do I lift it up to Jesus?
Or hold on with all my might?

I want to forgive
Yet hang on at the same time
I want Your forgiveness Lord
Yet what I feel is mine!

Peace beyond all measure
Only comes from Thee
By Your grace I yield to You
With You – let all anger flee

For it's by Your grace
I can freely forgive
And it's by Your mercy
In You – I can live

Forgiveness! Redemption!
What a gift divine
As I forgive others
Your forgiveness is mine!

"Help me Lord to make the choice that's right,
I know the choice is mine."

Rebecca A. Keefe
October 16, 2012

<u>Happy New Year</u>

Facing a brand new year brings with it a new hope and a new vision. We want to put the past in the past and start fresh. I often think of school with the big chalk boards displayed in front of the classroom. At the beginning of the day they are washed clean, nothing of yesterday remains. It's much the same with the New Year, a clean slate, something new to be written. At the same time, we worry about what could, would or should happen. This is where the Word of God is so precious and meaningful. Our Heavenly Father knows what we have needed of before we ask. What a wonderful thought and truth that is to realize and rejoice in. What better way to start the New Year than to just sit quietly after the commotion of the holidays and simply whisper the sweet name of Jesus. Shut yourself in with Him. It is a perfect way to begin the New Year. What do you think? Another thing may happen in that quiet time – you may even hear Him whispering back to you. There is power in the name of Jesus. You will never regret spending time in His presence.

Matthew 6:25-27, 32-34 (NLT)

So I tell you, don't worry about everyday life-whether you have enough food, drink, and clothes. Doesn't life consist of more than food and clothing?

Look at the birds. They don't need to plant or harvest or put food in barns because your heavenly Father feeds them. And you are far more valuable to him than they are.

Can all your worries add a single moment to your life: Of course not.

...Your heavenly Father already knows all your needs, and he will give you all you need from day to day if you live for him and make the Kingdom of God your primary concern.

So don't worry about tomorrow, for tomorrow will bring its own worries.

Happy New Year

Dear Lord,
It's a brand new year
I wonder what it will bring.
Will it cause my heart to fear
Or will it begin to sing?

Look no farther than today
Your Word tells us this is true
Leave the future in Your hands
Whether skies are Grey or Blue.

I know that trials are part of life
It's in them I learn to trust
Believe Your word and what You say
Wholeheartedly, it's a must!

So here I am on bended knee
Mistakes are in the past
I trust You fully as each day comes
With unwavering faith that will last.

But – if I waver from time to time

Whisper Jesus

You'll help me find the way
Coming back to You with a contrite heart
Standing strong, refusing to sway.

Who knows what lies beyond the bend
Or each turn the road may go
But You hold the world in Your hands
And You'll hold me, this I know!

For it's by Your Grace and Mercy
My walk in You remains strong
Trusting in Your Love and promises
I know I can never go wrong.

So in this brand New Year
No matter what comes my way
Help me Lord to always come to You
And hear what You have to say.

Bless this year and those I love
And those that don't love me
Let Your light shine brightly in my life
As I give this year to Thee.

Amen
Written by: Rebecca A. Keefe
January 8, 2013

He Brought Us Out

The story of the saving grace of our wonderful God never grows old for me! His plans for me never grow old. It is because of His great love that He brought me out of sin and showed me a new way of life with hope and promise. Remember when the kids were little and they'd have a favorite story? "Tell us the story again Mama! Read all the favorite parts!" They never tired of hearing their story told or read over and over. So it is with the story of salvation and redemption. "Tell me again, Father, why did you send your Son for me? Read me the favorite part of where He rose again!" "Tell me how you rescued the Israelites and brought them out of Egypt, so they could possess the Promised Land." I hope to my dying day I will always love to hear these stories and be able to apply them to my life. I pray I will always be able to tell the stories of Jesus as well. He truly brought us out that we may go in and possess the land He has prepared for us.

"Thank you God! And I can again Whisper Jesus." "Jesus, tell me again of Your love for me. Tell me why you love me so much."

Deuteronomy 6:20-23

In the future your children will ask you, "What is the meaning of these stipulations, laws and regulations that the LORD our God has given us?"
Then you must tell them, 'We were Pharaoh's slaves in Egypt, but the LORD brought us out of Egypt with amazing power.
Before our eyes the LORD brought us out of Egypt with amazing blows against Egypt and Pharaoh and all his people.
He brought us out of Egypt so he could give us this land he had solemnly promised to give our ancestors.'

Whisper Jesus

He Brought Us Out

He brought us out from there
That He might bring us in
He bought the bondage and the fear
And He forgave all our sin

The way we once knew
Filled with sorrow and strife
He brought us out of our sinful life
And He gave us a brand new life

'You shall rejoice' is
His promise so true
As you eat and remember
What He has done for you

The journey's not easy
He makes us strong as we stand
He equips with His tools
As we conquer this land

Never forget to remember
All He has done before
If we forget to remember
There will be no victories to score

You have brought us out
That You may bring us in
Your leading and guiding

Granting us strength to win!

Thank You Jesus!

Rebecca A. Keefe
April 2, 2013

I Am Amazed

It never ceases to amaze me that God loves me - that Jesus paid the price for my sins. As I was driving and singing these words came to me - could be a poem or a chorus. Simply put, I am amazed that God loves me, but I am so glad He does! Are you amazed with Jesus? Have you been able, in your busy, hectic life to find a quiet place to focus just on Him? It takes effort, and a resolve. Saying to you - this is "my" time with God, to focus on Him, to appreciate Him. "Jesus," "Jesus," "Jesus." I am amazed at Your love. As I whisper your name I am aware of Your sweet presence.
Thank You.

Luke 2:18 (NLT)

… and all who heard it were amazed at what the shepherds told them.

I Am Amazed

I am amazed my sweet Jesus
I'm amazed
I am amazed like the shepherds were
Who heard the angels sing
I am amazed that you came to earth
And of the message that You bring

I am amazed how You love me
That You died to set me free
I am amazed how You love me
Opened blind eyes that I might see
I am amazed how You love me
Not just for now but eternity

Whisper Jesus

I am amazed how you love me
How You restore my dignity

I am amazed how You love me
With love that reaches far and wide
How your love rushes over me
Like the roaring of the tide
I am amazed how You love me
How you whisper "Peace Be Still"
How you cause my heart to quiet
As I surrender to Your will

I am amazed my sweet Jesus
I'm amazed
I'm amazed

Rebecca A. Keefe
August 22, 2013

I Wonder

Whisper Jesus

When I read the story of David and Goliath and the mighty army of Israel and the Philistine army I smile because it shows how God does things differently. Once again the army of Israel is cowering in fear. Once again someone shows up and is willing to take on the challenge. What can a little shepherd boy do? Especially in the face of a loud, strong, menacing giant? Even if I was armed to the teeth so to speak, I still would be fearful to face such a ferocious enemy, an enemy who was loud and boastful but strong and mighty. Even David's brothers told him to go home and stop making a fool of himself.

Then there is the story of Esther whom God ordained to be in a certain place at a certain time just as he had David. Esther also was a woman who feared God and called her maidens to pray with her.

David had a righteous anger against the Philistines who were mocking Israel. God chose these two individuals to show us clearly that He just doesn't think like we do. Then I pray, "Oh Lord, that we would have their courage and their faith!"

Now consider this, perhaps God has you in this place, in this neighborhood, in this job, in this situation for just such a time as this. To use you as you seek Him, as an instrument of His love and mercy. Never be afraid to simply whisper Jesus when you are wondering what is going on and why you are here. He knows why and He will use you as you submit yourself to Him. Don't be afraid of the mean and nasty giants in your path or the powerful king. As you humble your heart before the King of kings, He will show you a way you never would have dreamed possible and will amaze you with how He works things out. Whisper Jesus and trust Him.

I Samuel 17:45 (NLT)

David shouted in reply (to Goliath), "You come to me with sword, spear, and javelin, but I come to you in the name of the LORD Almighty -- the God of the armies of Israel, whom you have defiled. Today the LORD will conquer you..."

Esther 4:14 (NLT)

If you keep quiet at a time like this, deliverance for the Jews will arise from some other place, but you and your relatives will die. What's more, who can say but that you have been elevated to the palace for just such a time as this?

I Wonder

Could I face a giant?
With 5 tiny little stones?
Would I wear the king's strong armor?
Or choose to tackle him alone?

I think I'd like protection
From the sword that he would swing
But God used David, gave him courage
Just to use his tiny little sling.

I wonder Lord,
With the giants that I face
Could you give me that same courage?
And slow down my rapid pace?

Whisper Jesus

Esther and David and
Numerous saints of old
Took off their own special armor as
you made them strong and bold.

Your Word says I can
You equip, so I will
Step out from among them
Hear Your Voice, and Be Still.

I wonder Lord, yet I know,
Your grace is sufficient for me
The giants I face will come tumbling down
As I listen and walk with Thee.

Rebecca A. Keefe
March 20, 2012

If I Could Picture Jesus

Whisper Jesus

This poem was inspired by asking if we would talk differently if Jesus was sitting at our kitchen table across from us. I also recall an old poem asking: If Jesus came to your house, I wonder what you'd do and the questions continue would we hide the magazines or turn off the radio or television. Would we change the music we might be playing? It's all about perspective isn't it? Often times the best place for me to pray and read or study is at my kitchen table. It's where I feel most comfortable. If you were to visit my home, the first thing I would do would be to invite you into my kitchen and make you a cup of tea or coffee. If I knew you were coming, I'd most likely bake a treat for us to share. Thus, the question still exists; if I could picture Jesus sitting across the table from me would it change how I do things? What about you, what would you do? Would I whisper His name or would I shout with joy that He had come to my house?

If I Could Picture Jesus

If I could picture Jesus
Sitting across the table from me
Would I offer Him some coffee
Or get Him a cup of tea

Would our conversation cover
My kids and their kids and more
Would He show me at my table
Time with Him is not a chore

He was a Friend to many
Even went to their homes to eat
Could I invite Him into my kitchen

Whisper Jesus

Giving Him the very best seat

And if He were truly here
In the flesh and not just spirit
Could I ask Him to explain to me
What is good and what has merit

I'm sure my demeanor would change
With Him sitting so close by
I may even thank Him for His love
As He wipes the tears from my eyes

But, I'm sure there would be laughter
As we look at my silly ways
And I'm sure He'd gently guide me
As we'd share His Word each day

I need to picture Jesus
Sitting across the table from me
I need to feel His presence
As He opens my eyes to see

He really is here in my kitchen
Or my bedroom or closet of prayer
Though I can't see Him in person
I know He is always there

He is my Friend and Savior
Forgiving and healing my soul
I know that He is with me
But I'd love to see Him more

So as I move throughout the day
Let me look at Your special chair
Sitting here at my table with me
As I come to You daily in prayer

Make it so Lord Jesus!

Rebecca A. Keefe

November 19, 2013

If I Could Turn Back Time

86

Whisper Jesus

Have you ever had an accident and wished you could have just 5 seconds back? Things would have been so different. Often we hear these words: "If I could turn back time!" I've said that a few times myself. Or we say things like: "I wish I hadn't said that!" Or perhaps we'd say, "Gosh! I wish I hadn't done that!" "I was so wrong!" This little poem expresses those thoughts. Sometimes we say "if I knew then what I know now, things could be so different." But who's to say we wouldn't make worse mistakes! You just never know.

We used to sing a song in Sunday school: "Be careful little mouth what you say, be careful little mouth what you say. For the Father up above is looking down in love. So be careful little mouth what you say." Of course it had other verses that went along with that too. Be careful little feet where you go. Be careful little eyes what you see. Be careful little hands what you do. You get the picture. We need to be careful because we cannot turn back time. Even though I cannot turn back time, I can find time to sit quietly and whisper the sweet Name of Jesus. I can ask Him to forgive me and cleanse my heart and renew my spirit. It is time well spent. As I sit quietly, breathe, and whisper "Jesus"

If I Could Turn Back Time

If I could turn back time
How different things would be.
A kinder word, a gentler touch.
A softer attitude for me.

The quick reply
That was really smart.

Whisper Jesus

The wandering eye,
That broke a heart.

To look back now
and say such things,
It's hard to tell
What life would bring.

So I will rely on You,
Sweet Lord of my life.
Who gives Grace and Mercy
Not a life filled with strife.

I will not look back
I will look ahead.
To life lived abundantly.
Not days filled with dread.

If I could turn back time
Who knows what life might be.
So I confess my sins,
And give them all to Thee.

Rebecca A. Keefe
November 15, 2011

If I Were King For The Day

Have you ever said those words? "If I were king for the day." I know I have! The news is full of injustices everywhere in the world. We look at things gone wrong in our society and we shake our heads. I am reminded of a scripture in Ecclesiastes 10 where it talks about things being backward. I often say in jest when we see something silly, "Now, that is just wrong in so many ways!" Yet, here again, things do seem backward, not the way that our good Lord intended. Maybe it's a good thing that He is in control. He is far more forgiving and loving and patient than I am. Praise the Lord! I don't need to be king for the day. But I certainly need my King of kings to order my day. And if I can stop and simply Whisper Jesus along the way, I may not be so judgmental. What about you?

Ecclesiastes 10:5-7 (NLT)

There is another evil I have seen as I have watched the world go by. Kings and rulers make a grave mistake
if they give foolish people great authority, and if they fail to give people of proven worth their rightful place of dignity.
I have even seen servants riding like princes – and princes walking like servants.

If I Were King For The Day

We often say in joking
If I were king for the day
There'd be a lot of people
Who'd really have to pay!

Whisper Jesus

If I were judge and saw
The guilty cross my path
I'm afraid I'd have no mercy
As I showed to them my wrath!

So I guess it's my good fortune
To be not judge or king
But give it all to Jesus
And let him, the justice bring!

He heals all our transgressions
Wipes all our sins away
He took them all to Calvary
Gives new hope for every day

Thank You Jesus!

Rebecca A. Keefe
April 17, 2012

<u>In Him</u>

This poem was written after studying how to become stronger in the Lord. We so often try to find strength to face life in general in ourselves. So many times all we need to do is simply spend time – precious time – being quiet before the Lord. Shutting off all social devices; no phone, no computer, no television, no radio - just sitting in quietness. Years ago we used to have a little silver child's cup that had an inscription on it that said: "Sometimes I sits and thinks and sometimes I just sits." In today's day and age, even at age 71, I find it hard to just sit and think or just sit. Yet, this is just exactly what our Lord wants us to do. "Come away with me," He calls. "Just sit awhile and be refreshed." Just like the Song of Solomon 2:10 and 13 records: "Rise up, my beloved, my fair one, and come away." "Lord, help me to do just that today." Perhaps this is the morning I will sit quietly and simply whisper "Jesus."

Acts 17:28 (NIV)

For in him we live and move and have our being.

Song of Solomon 2:10 & 13

"Rise up, my beloved, my fair one, and come away."

In Him

O Lord, Your Word is so clear
That my strength is in YOU alone
Though sometimes I worry and complain
Not bringing my cares to Your throne

Whisper Jesus

In You – not me – In You
It seems to take me so long to see
Coming to You is the answer
Trusting in You and not in me

But when I can quietly meditate
Leaving the world behind
And sit in Your sweet presence
Letting You sweep over my mind

Quieting all my rambled thoughts
Allowing Your Spirit to draw near
It's then I see Your strength is mine
As once again I lose my fear

You are my shield of protection
You give ear to my heart's deepest cry
In You there is grace and glory
And in You my spirit can fly

You give me Hope in fragile places
Where there is fear and worry and pain
You show me time spent in Your presence
Will grant me - Your peace - to gain

It's in You and with You alone
Time spent is never wasted
For You give grace and glory
And it's of Your goodness I've tasted

Whisper Jesus

No good thing will You withhold
To those who walk upright
I place my trust in you completely
For You Are my strength and might.

Make it so Lord Jesus!

Rebecca A. Keefe
March 18, 2014

Is It Kind – Is It Necessary – Is It True?

Growing up in a large family produces tons of stories. We love to listen as well as recount stories of people, places and things. Every once in a while my mom would remind us kids that we should have a guideline to our storytelling. She would remind us that our Grandpa Rice used to have three guidelines to relating a story. Is it kind? Is it necessary? Is it true? Our response would be, "Oh man! Now we can't talk about anybody!" But, isn't that the way it is? We love a good story. The news is full of all kinds of stories. Some true, some not so true. What about our conversation? Can we honestly answer these three questions? I confess I have to bridle my tongue and ask God to help me. What about you? Am I just rattling off at the mouth or does what I say have value? Whew! "Lord help us! Lord help me! And again, Lord, as I Whisper "Jesus" I am made keenly aware of Your sweet presence. That tempers everything. Let the stories I tell center around You and Your love."

James 1: 26 and 3:8-9 (NIV)

1:26 if anyone considers himself religious and yet does not keep a tight rein of his tongue, he deceives himself and his religion is worthless.

3:8-9 but no man can tame the tongue. It is a restless evil, full of deadly poison. With the tongue we praise our Lord and Father, and with it we curse men, who have been made in God's likeness

Is It Kind – Is It Necessary – Is It True

We all love a good story

Whisper Jesus

With lots of drama and such
With all the scary details
We just can't get too much

Then Mom would remind us
Of what Grandpa used to say
Ask these three questions
Then tell others what you may

Is it kind?
Does it tell a nice story?
Will it hurt or build up
Bring disgrace or bring glory?

Is it necessary?
Does it need to be told?
Are you just telling tales?
Are you being too bold?

Is it true?
What are you honestly saying?
Can you tell this story?
As if you were praying?

What a spoil sport
She seemed to be
Then I can't talk about anyone
Unless I talk truthfully about me!

Would Jesus Approve?
Does He hear what I say?

Whisper Jesus

Is it kind, necessary and true
This changes everything – perhaps I should pray!

Please forgive me Lord!
For the times I spoke out of place
Help cover my mouth
With Your love and your grace.

Rebecca A. Keefe
June 2014

It's A Beautiful Day In The Neighborhood

The Book of Revelation is not only prophetic and interesting, it is scary as well. The more I read it, the more I think I need a revelation to read the Book of Revelation! This is what prompted this poem as we were attempting lessons in Revelation in the Ladies Bible Study. Let me invite you to open the scriptures today. Just sit in a quiet place with a cup of coffee or tea, and begin to read. Before you read, let me encourage you once again, just Whisper Jesus. As you read, begin to think about what you are reading. If you are using a Bible with study guides, read those guides as well. Ask our sweet Lord to open your understanding. There is a little word used many times in the Psalms. It is the word, Selah. Simply put, it means, stop and think about that. As we read the scripture we need to do just that. Stop. Think about what we are reading. We are not in a contest to see how fast we can read or how much we can read. We just need to read. Then stop and think about it. How long has it been since you've done that? If it's been awhile, let me encourage you to do that today. Right now, read, stop, think and while you're in a quiet place – Whisper Jesus.

Revelation 1: 3 and 13:10-12 (NLT)

God blesses the one who reads this prophecy to the church, and he blesses all who listen to it and obey what it says. For the time is near when these things will happen.

Then I heard a loud voice shouting across the heavens, "It has happened at last – the salvation and power and kingdom of our God and the authority of his Christ! For the Accuser has been thrown

down to earth – the one who accused our brothers and sisters before our God day and night.
And they have defeated him because of the blood of the Lamb and because of their testimony. And they were not afraid to die.
Rejoice O heavens! And you who live in the heavens, rejoice!

It's A Beautiful Day in the Neighborhood

It's a beautiful day in the neighborhood
It's a scary one as well.......

Sometimes I'd like a poster that
Would tell me which way to go
Then I read Revelation and say
Wow! I just don't want to know!

Great battles in the future
In the present and in the past
Makes me really wonder
Just how long they'll last!

From the beginning to the end
We know Who is in charge
Though the dragon and the beast
Look so very very large

Even though my understanding
Seems so very dim
One thing I am sure of
Is that my Faith's secure in Him!

Whisper Jesus

And yet I find I'm fearful
When I see what may lay ahead
I pray His perfect Peace will keep me
From all fear and dread

From Genesis to Revelation
Filled with victories and loss
Yet Jesus conquered all the fight
When He rose up from the Cross!

It's a beautiful day in the neighborhood
It's a scary one as well
But we fight with Holy Armor
And our enemy is bound for Hell!

Thank You Jesus!

Rebecca A. Keefe
January 15, 2013

It's All About You

Nehemiah was given a huge task to do. He was given the equipment, the resources, the manpower, and the help he needed to complete this awesome task of rebuilding walls of Jerusalem. He had a vision of what needed to be done. But he was not doing this for his glory or his own ambition. From the very beginning he sought God and asked for His guidance and help. He did not go out on his own. It was amazing that all that work was accomplished in just fifty-two days!

All throughout the Bible we see record after record of how God does amazing and great things through his people who trust Him wholly. People like you and me who come to God with whatever task is at hand, asking for divine help. Those who know us will be able to see that truly God is with us. It must be God working in the situation. It's not about us, but about the power of God working in us. "Truly Lord, It's all about You!" If I happen to lose focus, I can Whisper Jesus and it will come back into place again. For His name is powerful and can turn us around from going in the wrong direction. His name can also cause the devil to flee. Whisper Jesus for it is all about Him and His great love.

Nehemiah 6:15 & 16 (NLT)

So on October 2 the wall was finally finished-just fifty two days after we had begun.
When our enemies and the surrounding nations heard about it….They realized that this work had been done with the help of our God.

Whisper Jesus

It's All About You

O Lord, help me to listen
Before starting a work for You.
There's so much to do to get started
Yet I need a plan from You.

So much of the work is all about me
My ability, my call, my goals
But this time I need to listen to You
As you show me which way to go.

There are so many voices to listen to
What advice should I give or receive
Remove the rubble or build the wall
In whose counsel should I believe?

You've given me helpers along the way
I don't have to do it alone
But there will be those in the path ahead
Who will have a heart of stone.

Not to be swayed by lies and deceit
Not to be fooled or dismayed
Open my eyes to their tricky plans
As Your plan to me is displayed

It's not about me Sweet Jesus
It's all about You and Your plan
I give you control to do what You will
To listen to You and not man.

Nehemiah felt led to build a wall and gates
Joshua prayed for Jericho's to fall
They led the people on their quest
But first on Your Name they would call.

Tools and swords and guards close by
Each man guarded his home each day
Attention was on the work to be done
This was not a time to play.

The enemy of our souls will always try
To destroy and defeat all man
But You show us in such unusual ways
It's all about You and Your plan!

Rebecca A. Keefe
May 22, 2012

It's Christmas Time Again

I am guilty of forgetting the true reason we celebrate Christmas Day. I love to decorate the house with Nutcrackers inherited from my mother. I bake a ton of Italian cookies to give away as gifts, as well as munch-on through the holidays. I love looking at the decorations in the neighborhood and just enjoy the festivities. I love to get the family together to make a dish we call by a nickname "Kaplit". It is Cappeletti – like ravioli but cooked in chicken and beef broth. Homemade noodle dough stuffed with all kinds of tasty meats and cheeses! It is easy to get caught up in all the commotion both good and bad that happens during the holidays. One of my favorite figurines is called The Kneeling Santa. It is Santa kneeling at baby Jesus in the manger. There is a tune within that little figurine that plays "O Come Let Us Adore Him." It is a visual reminder of what Christmas is all about. Where, as the scripture says, "every knee shall bow and every tongue shall confess that Jesus Christ is Lord" (Romans 14:11). The birth of our precious Lord and Savior is why we celebrate. As this poem states, "may the love of Jesus fill your heart" not only at Christmas but each day and each hour of the year. I am sure the shepherds whispered the Name of Jesus in awe too. Let me invite you to do the same as you think about the awesomeness of it all - Just Whisper Jesus. "Jesus" "Jesus" "Jesus"

It's Christmas time Again

Isaiah 9:6

For unto us a Child is born, unto us a Son is given; and the government will be upon His shoulder. And His Name will be called Wonderful, Counselor, Mighty God, Everlasting Father, Prince of Peace

It's Christmas time again
With all its excitement and fuss
The lights shining bright on every house
And presents wrapped up like a truss

My little tree has an angel on top
Reminding me of what Christmas really is
God's gift to me and gift to you
Giving a gift that was truly His

For unto us a Child is born,
Unto us a Son is given;
A wonderful unspeakable gift
That my sins and yours be forgiven

And His Name will be called
Wonderful, Counselor, Mighty God,
We look at this gift, so precious from God
And we are speechless and truly awed.

Everlasting Father, Prince of Peace
words that are rare these days
Yet God's promise is sure and true

Whisper Jesus

For that we can truly praise

It's Christmas time again
Joy, Peace, Hope for the Lost
Time to slow down and ponder
God's gift to us at great Cost
No one is perfect except our Lord
He takes all our sins away
He came as a babe in Bethlehem
The true reason we have Christmas Day

So Merry Christmas to you and yours
Let's rejoice this Christmas Day
May the Love of Jesus fill your heart
Is my prayer for you today.

Rebecca A. Keefe
December 24, 2013

Jesus is the Reason

Isaiah 9:6
For unto us a Child is born, unto us a Son is given; and the government will be upon His shoulders and His Name will be called Wonderful, Counselor, Mighty God, Everlasting Father, Prince of Peace

"O Lord, You truly are the reason for my existence. Where would I be without You in my life? The fact that You came to earth to die for my sins is beyond my comprehension. Thank You! But to know that it does not end there is even more remarkable. You came not only to die, but to offer real Hope, and Peace and Healing. You also are preparing a Home in Heaven not only for me, but for those who confess you as Lord and Savior. You are truly the Reason for the Season – not only at Christmas, but for every season of our lives. Again Lord, Thank You! I stand in awe of your birth, your life, your sacrifice. Thank You My sweet Jesus! Thank You! Help me never ever forget – that You, Jesus, are the reason for the season. And help me whisper Jesus softly and quietly in the midst of the holiday rush. Finding a solemn time to simply Whisper Jesus"

Jesus is the Reason

I know Jesus is the Reason
But I've got so much to do!
The tree to trim and toys to buy
Cards from me to you!

Whisper Jesus

I love to see the children
And hear the holiday songs
I love the entertaining and all
But not the holiday throngs!

Yes, I know it's all about Jesus
But then I get carried away
I forget about the manger
How he was laid upon the hay

I forget the angels announcing
Our Saviors birth behind the Inn
Born in a lowly stable
Come to take away our sin!

I forget about Mary and Joseph
The wise men who followed the star
Shepherds who saw the angels
Announcing Jesus close by and afar

I know Jesus is the Reason
We celebrate Christmas Day
Slow me down sweet Jesus
Forgive my busyness I pray

It's nice to celebrate family
Give gifts and kisses and all
We'd be so lost without You
If You hadn't died for all

Your birth, death, and resurrection

Whisper Jesus

Is what gives us Hope, Joy and Peace
Your intercession for our sins
Granting Mercy that will never cease

Thank you Dear Father in Heaven
for the Gift of your precious Son
It's because of Him I can live forever
And the battle over sin is won

So in this holiday season
of laughter and giving and mirth
Let's remind one another gently
It's because of our Saviors birth

Jesus is truly the Reason
We have cause to rejoice today
Let's spread The Good News He is Risen
And our sins He has taken away!

Merry Christmas!
Rebecca A. Keefe
December 11, 2012

Joy and Peace

There are times in our lives when there simply is no joy and peace of any kind. Our hearts and emotions are in turmoil! Everything is topsy turvy. Nothing seems right. This can happen even when we are right in the center of God's Will. We come against battles that we don't understand. The people in our lives, the jobs we work in, even our pets may become ill. Peace and joy can escape us. Yet, this is where the concept of the peace that comes from God which passes all understanding comes into play. As we go to the scripture and begin to read it out loud we can begin to rest in the Lord. Is it easy? No. But, it helps to recognize we may just need to slow down a bit, and like Mary, come and sit at the feet of Jesus for a bit. It will help calm the troubled heart as we lean closer into Him. He knows our need before we even ask. He can whisper "Shhhh" to our hearts and restore the peace to our being. Whisper Jesus. He will hear our whisper and restore us completely. And if we stay quiet, we may even hear Him whisper softly to us.

John 14:27(NIV)

Peace I leave with you, My peace I give to you; not as the world gives do I give to you. Let not your heart be troubled, neither let it be afraid.

Psalm 30:5 (NIV)

......Weeping may endure for a night, But joy comes in the morning.

Whisper Jesus

Joy and Peace

Have I lost my Joy?
Have I lost my Peace?
Is it true that You give
Peace and Joy that won't cease?

How do I find it?
Where do I begin?
Does it come from without?
Or does it start from within?

Joy unspeakable,
Yes that is true.
It comes from the Father
And it starts Lord, with You.

Peace like a river
So calm and so sweet
I find it, Sweet Jesus
When I sit at Your feet.

Rebecca A. Keefe
May 29, 2012

Legacy

It never fails – every time I go to a funeral or memorial service for someone who has passed, I come away thinking how short life is. As I hear the kind words of the loved ones who are left behind I always wonder what kind of legacy I will leave behind.

I want my children, now adults, to remember their Mom as someone who loved them with all her heart. Also, that I am sorry I could not shield them from each harm and hurt this old world serves up.

And I want them to know that I pray for them almost daily. I want them to know that when I pray, I am convinced that I am praying to a loving God who is real and relevant. I not only love them but God is very much a part of my existence. I am a lover of God.

Growing up as a young girl in Indiana (and many other states) I became aware of Jesus and invited Him to come into my heart and life. I also learned that He was my best Friend who I could talk to constantly about everything, good or bad, sad or happy.

Having a father who was addicted to alcohol was not easy. After he returned from World War II having fought and survived the battle at Normandy he was never the same. When he was drinking he could become violent and we all feared him. He died from alcoholism when he was 56 and left a legacy of a broken life behind. He was gifted in writing poetry and songs. But a lot of his poetry was dark and revealed a troubled heart. When he was trying to walk with God his songs reflected his love for God as well. His family was left with mixed feelings about his giftedness and his weaknesses and his endless struggle with drinking. It also stretched my prayer life at a very young age.

My mother on the other hand was a saint. At least in my opinion she was. Was she perfect? Not by any means! But she loved her kids and worked for thirty plus years as a cashier at Kroger's supermarket supporting us so we'd never have to go hungry. She had no car and walked to work or took the bus, and always, always prayed as she walked. She left behind an example to follow. She was not only my Mom, but my confidant, my prayer partner and my very good friend. She always asked the question: "Becky, Have you prayed about it?" referring to any problem I would share with her.

When I die, which could be anytime, I truly want to be remembered as a woman who was a lover of God and who loved her children and grandchildren and her faithful husband, and her siblings with a fierce love.

Looking back we can always see things we coulda, woulda, shoulda done. But God knows as we grow – we do try – and God knows also – that we fail at some things too. I am not perfect by any means. I have made some terrible choices and terrible mistakes in the course of my 70 plus years! There was no fairy tale marriage to my children's father. I can't leave them the kind of legacy of a perfect, blissful marriage. I could write millions of thoughts on that subject, but tonight, I am just "thoughting." If I were to pass away in my sleep tonight, what would I want my family to remember? I would want them to remember that I am passionate about my love for them, that I am passionate about my love for God. That I am convinced that Christ has forgiven all my sins and mistakes, and that

He has prepared a home in heaven for me. I pray with all my heart that each one of my children, and their wives, husbands and children will also come to know Jesus as Lord and Savior - which nothing else matters.

What can I say? I am a lover of God, I love my family, I love my husband who is my true friend along with Jesus!

Rebecca A. Keefe
September 14, 2013

Legacy

Today I attended a funeral
Of a friend who had passed away
It always causes me to wonder
When I die, what will people say?

What kind of legacy do I leave?
Will I be remembered for any good I've done
Or will they remember the times I failed
And not all battles fought were won

I want them to remember
That Jesus is my dearest Friend
That I'm passionate about my love for Him
Knowing His love for me never ends

So many things are temporary
They grow old and fall apart
Except for the Love of Jesus

Whisper Jesus

He never leaves us nor departs

I want my kids to remember
Nobody loves them more than me
Outside of the love of Jesus
Who died to set us free

I want them to remember that
My love has never grown old
As they grow and mature in life
Even in not doing what they were told

My love has not been conditional
From the time they were first conceived
I've prayed and committed them to God's care
And prayed His love they'd receive

And of the people that I've taught
I pray they have seen God's love
Telling not so much of who I am
That His Peace descends like a dove

Of my husband I know he'll remember
The times we have laughed and cried
The times we have trusted God together
When each other's tears we have dried

The times we sat in the hot tub
Shared our coffee and plans for the day
The times we caught snowflakes on our tongues
And held hands in the water and prayed

Whisper Jesus

This is what I hope they'll remember
As they say their last goodbye
Outside of them I love Jesus
And He'll wipe all tears from their eyes

He's the one who will never fail them
Will never leave them alone or unloved
Absent from the body and present with God
In the arms of my Beloved

Rebecca A. Keefe
October 2013

<u>Let Go and Let God</u>

It's hard to just let go of something we value. It's difficult to trust something precious to someone else. How many times have we heard that phrase "Just Let Go!." I've often said: "We want what we want when we want it, and we want it right now!." The disciples were in a dilemma. They forgot about Who they had in the boat with them. All of a sudden a big storm hit. The peace and serenity they had just experienced a short while before that was immediately destroyed. They feared they would perish. And when they asked Jesus if he cared, then He showed them the impossible. He spoke to the winds and the waves and said, "Peace, Be still" and much to their amazement and joy the winds and the waves ceased. Wow! First they asked how he could sleep all covered up cozy and comfy and then they asked how He could speak to the storm and cause it to stop. Amazing! In our lives when the peace we hold so dear is gone we can cry out to Jesus. He alone can bring peace as we let go and let God do His thing instead of ours. It's so much easier that way! We need to remember that He is still in the boat with us. We can cry out in fear or we can simply whisper His Name in the storm. "Jesus" "Jesus" "Jesus" It is then He will show us that He is still in control of the winds and waves and the troubles in our lives as well. We serve such an awesome God!

Mark 4:39 (NKJV)

And he arose, and rebuked the wind, and said unto the sea, Peace, be still. And the wind ceased, and there was a great calm.

I like this translation also in:

Mark 4:39 (NASB)

And He got up and rebuked the wind and said to the sea, "Hush, be still." And the wind died down and it became perfectly calm.

Let Go and Let God

We've heard it said
"Let Go and Let God"
Let Him work in the places
On which we have trod.

But most of the time
We hang on too long
And instead of sweet Peace
We soon lose our song.

If we hang onto God
Letting go of our will
We'll then hear His whisper
of "Peace be Still"

Rebecca A. Keefe
May 7, 2013

Whisper Jesus

<u>Listen – Look – Believe</u>

I have often wondered why we won't believe God and His promises unless it is written in stone, proof positive that the promise is real. Abraham and Sarah were given a promise by God Himself. Yet, they looked at what they could see, just themselves, aged and worn out and beyond childbearing years. But God could see beyond the outward and could see the fulfillment of His promise. All He asked for was Abraham to believe His Word. Trust. Believe. Wait. God has so much more in store for us if would Listen – Look – Believe. In order for us to do this we have to stop rushing around so much. Sometimes it is just sitting quietly, with no interference whatsoever and simply whispering "Jesus." Once we are quiet we will be able to listen. The reverse can happen also. Perhaps we will hear God's soft voice whispering back to us, speaking into the depths of our hearts.

Genesis 15:5 & 6 (NASB)

And He took him outside and said, "Now look toward the heavens, and count the stars, if you are able to count them." And He said to him, "So shall your descendants be."
Then he believed in the LORD; and He reckoned it to him for righteousness.

Galatians 6:3 (NASB)

Even so Abraham BELIEVED GOD, AND IT WAS RECKONED TO HIM AS RIGHTEOUSNESS.

Hebrews 11:1 (NASB)

Now faith is the assurance of things hoped for, the conviction of things not seen.

Hebrews 11:8 (NASB)

By faith Abraham, when he was called, obeyed going...

Hebrews 11:11 (NASB)

By faith even Sarah herself received the ability to conceive

Genesis 15 – Galatians 3:6 – Hebrews 11

Listen – Look – Believe

Abraham listened as God spoke
Words of promise about his heir
For he and Sarah were barren
No offspring of theirs to share

God promised to be a Shield to him
Saying his reward would be very great
But Abraham asked 'to whom would it go'
Since having a child seemed too late

Yet God had a surprise in store for him
As he told him to look to the sky
'Your heirs will be like the stars in heaven
For I am answering your hearts' cry'

Whisper Jesus

And Abraham believed the LORD
As by faith he listened and looked
He knew God would make it happen
As God's Word he gladly took

And it's just like that for me and you
As we listen, look and believe
God's Word is sure and unfailing
As by faith we step out and receive

We sell ourselves short when we fail to see
By faith what the future holds
God's promises are Yea and Amen
As Time and the Ages unfold

God's Word shows us great examples
Those who trusted when all seemed lost
Overcoming giants and enemies
Following Him no matter the cost

We battle unbelief and fear
As the devil whispers hateful lies
Yet we know that God is faithful
He draws near and hears our cries

We can look to the world for answers
We can trust others who will fail
But, let us be like Abraham and Sarah
Believing God's covenant would prevail

Whisper Jesus

Thank you Lord for Your loving-kindness
For Your patience with our frail frame
Thank You for Your promise in Jesus
Who is with us and forever the same!

Rebecca A. Keefe
February 4, 2014

Live It – Act It – No Complaining

Our pastor at Bethany Assembly of God urges us all to begin each New Year in fasting, fasting not only from food, if we feel lead, but also fast from complaining and grumbling. The challenge is to fast for 21 days. This can prove to be a challenge! We ask each other if we are merely stating an opinion or if we are, in fact, complaining. Thus, this poem was born. The best way to get my mind off of complaining is to take the focus off me, myself and I. The best way to do that is simply whisper the Name of Jesus, quietly, prayerfully and reverently. You will see a change in your attitude. I guarantee it. Try it!

Live It – Act It – No Complaining

Can I really live it
And not grumble for one day?
Can I live a Christ filled life
Being careful what I say?

Grandpa used to teach us
Be careful the words you use.
The words you say can build one up
Or cause a lasting bruise.

How you act not what you say
Is most important child.
Live like Jesus, walk His way
And let your words be mild.

Okay Lord, it's just me and You.

Whisper Jesus

Show me how to act and what to do.
The end result should be the same
Bringing honor and glory to Your name.

By Your grace Lord,
Actions it will be.
No words of complaining
Will be coming from me!

Rebecca A. Keefe
January 17, 2012

Looking at Another New Year

It seems I always get sentimental at another new year, at a wedding or a funeral or a family reunion, it must be the Italian in me. I always wonder how things will be in the future as well as reconciled from the past. Resolutions, promises, failed resolutions, failed promises. These all accompany my thoughts on looking at another new year. Plus, it amazes me how fast time flies. I once remarked to my teenage granddaughter that I felt as young on the inside as her Mama was on the outside. She looked at me and said, "Oh Nanny! You are so silly!" I wasn't trying to be funny. I really meant it! So what does another year hold for us? We don't know! But God does and that is all that matters because He holds us in the palm of His hand. We keep ourselves in the race. The apostle Paul says it quite well in the following scripture. After encountering Jesus he was never the same. So it is with us, encountering Jesus is a life changing event. We are never the same. We begin to run a new race in the sweet name of Jesus. When is the last time you allowed yourself to be quiet? Not saying a word to anyone, not listening to anyone or anything. Perhaps now would be a good time to do that. And in the quietness, simply whisper "Jesus."

Philippians 3:12 - 14 (NLT)

I don't mean to say that I have already achieved these things or that I have already reached perfection! But I keep working toward that day when I will finally be all that Christ Jesus saved me for and wants me to be.
No, dear brothers and sisters, I am still not all I should be, but I am focusing all my energies on this one thing: Forgetting the past and looking forward to what lies ahead.

Whisper Jesus

I strain to reach the end of the race and receive the prize for which God, through Christ Jesus, is call us up to heaven.

Looking at Another New Year

At the beginning of this new year
Looking back and forward at the same time
How did the seconds and minutes disappear
Days slipping away as each hour chimes

My eyes go to failed promises
Then my heart goes back to Thee
You've forgiven all my transgressions
And cast them into Your deepest sea

It's so easy to make new resolutions
To vow to do better each day
Yet in my humanity I know I will fail
Unless I come to God and pray

It's Your strength that takes my weakness
And my sinful nature as well
It's Your Hope that gives me Peace
And Your grace my fears dispel

A new year with fresh resolutions
It's what we do as the New Year appears
Looking forward to each new day
Looking back perhaps with tears

Lord, I wonder what this new year will hold

Whisper Jesus

Laughter-sorrow-sickness-health
Restless or at peace with You
Trusting You with life itself

You are my Hope for days to come
Each one with its joy or sorrow
You are my Peace both day and night
Giving me Grace to face tomorrow

Successes and failures all wrapped in one
As we view the year as a whole
May they spur us on and give new resolve
As we focus on each new goal

But most of all Dear Lord I pray
Let my mind be turned towards Thee
Trusting You to tenderize my heart
Focusing on others and not just on me

Lead me Sweet Jesus by Your hand
Holy Spirit sweep over my soul
Let this New Year bring honor to You
Loving You more my only goal

Looking back and looking forward
Placing the past and future in Your care
What a joy to know you take charge of it all
Assured by Your Word You are there

Thank you Sweet Lord
For This New Year 2014!

Whisper Jesus

Rebecca A. Keefe
January 2, 2014

<u>Looking For Love</u>

Where do you look for love? Where do we find love? What is love? We use the word "love" so liberally in our conversation. I love that dress! I love that house! I love that puppy! I love that show! The list is endless of all the things we love. What about true love? What about God's redeeming love? In my opinion, we all have void places in our lives at one time or another. We look to one another or to activities or anything close by that could help fill that void. When we lose a loved one, or a position, or a friend, or something of great value, we have a void. It's so easy to gravitate to the easiest way to fill that void. When in reality, God is the one who can fill every void and meet every need as we come to Him with an open heart. No matter what empty space we have in our lives there is One who is the Great Example of Love. It is Jesus Christ. He is the greatest example of true love because He gave His life for you and me.

"As I come to you in this quiet hour Lord, all I can do is Whisper Jesus. I have no words to say except Your Name. Jesus. Jesus. Jesus. You are the true lover of my soul. Please show me sweet Jesus how I can remain in Your love."

John 15:9-15 (NLT)

I have loved you even as the Father has loved me. Remain in my love.
When you obey me, you remain in my love, just as I obey my Father and remain in his love.
I have told you this so that you will be filled with my joy. Yes, your joy will overflow!

Whisper Jesus

I command you to love each other in the same way that I love you.
And here is how to measure it – the greatest love is shown when
people lay down their lives for their friends.
You are my friends if you obey me.
I no longer call you servants, because a master doesn't confide in his
servants. Now you are my friends, since I have told you everything
the Father told me.

Looking For Love

Looking for love
In all the wrong places
When it's only God
Who fills broken spaces

My friends are great
Showing quality care
But only sweet Jesus
My burdens will bear

My family is special
As they share their love
Yet love everlasting
Comes from God up above

His love is forever
His word always true
He can take the black clouds
And turn them to blue

He takes all my failings

Whisper Jesus

My mistakes and my fall
Covering them with His mercy
And erasing them all

His love everlasting
His promises sure
His joy is endless
And His grace will endure

Sometimes I lose focus
Grabbing someone close by
When I should reach for Jesus
Raise my face to the sky

I need to turn to Him fully
Accepting His grace
Walking strong in His presence
Running fit in Life's race

Complete in the knowledge
Nothing can pull us apart
Loving Jesus and others
As He enlarges my heart

"So be it Lord,
Help me look for Your divine Love
In every avenue of my life."
Amen

Rebecca A. Keefe
May 14, 2013

<u>Looking Through A Glass Darkly</u>

Have you ever tried to look at your reflection in a mirror in the dark? What you see is barely visible. It's like that when we try to figure things out for ourselves sometimes, especially a hard issue. We can barely see the outline of the issue, yet we know it's there. This is when the Lord tells us to be still so we can hear His voice. Just wait a bit. That is hard for me because I don't have a lot of patience. It is so hard to sit quietly when there is turmoil bubbling inside and outside as well. It takes extreme effort to apply the following scripture of "be still." As I Whisper Jesus, I ask him to help me be still, for I cannot still my anxious thoughts without His divine help. I cannot wait patiently for him, unless He helps me wait. And I can only do this as I stop, and Whisper, "Jesus."

Psalm 37:7 (NIV)

Be still before the LORD and wait patiently for him.

Looking Through a Glass Darkly

Straining at the bit I seem to be
Trying to see what there is to see

Looking through a glass darkly
Exactly what does it mean?

In a room very dimly lit
Like looking through a dark screen

I think I see the road to take

Whisper Jesus

And yet I falter still

Teach me Jesus not to quake
Instead - obey thy words "Be Still"

Written by Rebecca A. Keefe
March 22, 2011

Lord I Confess

Why do you suppose we try to hide things? It's been said that if we try to hide something – there must be something sideways about it. A good secret is hiding a nice surprise, but most times, a secret involves what my husband would call "skullduggery." There is a reason we try to hide things: perhaps shame or embarrassment. When my children were small and it was suddenly quiet, I knew it meant they were up to something! I would ask them what they were doing. Their reply was most always, "Nothing," which was not true. Whenever I would come into the room to investigate they would try to hide whatever it was they were up to. Secrets! Hide it from Mom at all costs! It's the guilt that gives it away. My Mom would always make us look her straight in the eye if she suspected we were lying. Somehow our eyes told the truth no matter how hard we tried to look innocent, much like our spiritual lives. We might as well 'fess up' because God knows it all anyway! Like the scripture we reference for this poem: "Finally, I confessed my sins to you and stopped trying to hide them." What a wonderful privilege we have in our relationship with God. He forgives us over and over and hears our cry for help! For the gross mistakes I have made, bad decisions, wrong relationships, unfaithfulness, He forgives! When I truly repent, He forgives. Repentance comes, however, after a time of quiet. When I have had a chance to see where I have been, and where I am headed. When I repent and confess my sins, He forgives me! Sometimes it is because I have simply and earnestly whispered "Jesus" in my prayer. I John 1:9; "If we confess our sins, He is able and just to forgive our sins, and cleanse us from all unrighteousness." How blessed we are! Jesus, sweet Jesus, thank You!

Psalm 32:5 (NLT)

Finally, I confessed all my sins to You and stopped trying to hide them. I said to myself, "I will confess my rebellion to the LORD. " And You forgave me! All my guilt is gone.

Lord, I Confess

You touch my life with sweetness
And wipe away all my tears
You tell me that You love me
And take away all my fears

Dear Lord, I am so unworthy
Yet You remove all my sin
I confess my faithless actions
Please, come and dwell within

I love you dear Lord Jesus
You are more precious than gold
More costly than fine diamonds
Your sacrifice, a value untold

I confess I still get angry
Over wrongs that have been done
I'd wipe my enemies off the earth
But it's Your battle to be fought and won

Yet, Lord, with this I wonder
How do I handle it all
I'd shun those who shun me

Whisper Jesus

But, it's on You I need to call

You see the struggle within me
I'm so prone to do things my way
Forgive, Dear Father in heaven
Please show me what to do and say

I praise You for your mercy
Your ways so much higher than mine
So I humbly yield my spirit
By Your grace not my will but Thine

I confess I love you Jesus
You are all the world to me
Take my hand, walk beside me
Give me eyes to see what You see

Make it so, Sweet Jesus

Rebecca A. Keefe
August 14, 2013

Lord Teach Me Your Ways

This poem was inspired by Pastor Richard Adams' sermon on the Power of Forgiveness. As he preached I was reminded of others beside Moses and David, Daniel, the three Hebrew men and many others who had a vision of who God was. And I am reminded again, that God's ways are not our ways. That's why it is so important to become familiar with God's Word that portrays many stories of men and women who followed God and believed His Word. They tackled extremely hard, overwhelming circumstances and were shown over and over that God would win the battle, but not on their terms - on His terms and His ways.

I miss it sometimes because I am so short-sighted. Plus, I keep trying to figure out things myself. It is only as I come to my wits end sometimes, that I give in and say "Here it is Lord Jesus, please sharpen my heart and mind for your sake. Help me to be quiet before I get myself all worked up about people, places and things. Help me Lord, to simply whisper Your Name. Jesus."

Lord Teach Me Your Ways

Moses in the scripture asked
"LORD, teach me your ways"
Am I so brave as to ask the same
And listen to what You say?

If I truly learn God's ways
Adjust my ways to His Will
And if I truly learn His ways
Will I love Him still?

David was anointed king
Twenty years before it came to pass
He had his vision of who You were
Faithful and Just to the last

I think of Daniel as he prayed
Being warned not to pray to You
He's thrown into a lion's den
With nothing but darkness in view

Yet You sent an angel to Daniel
In the midst of that cold dark den
You shut the mouths of the lions
As You breathed Your peace on them

Shadrach, Meshach, and Abed-Nego
Who refused to bow down to the king
Faced a fiery furnace for their acts
As the Son of Man stood ministering

In the middle You appeared in the fire
Right next to Your faithful three
You showed You'd stand beside them
As they vowed only love for Thee

Lord You try to get our attention
By showing Your power in the weak
You're with us in famine and in wealth
You show Your love to the meek

Whisper Jesus

Can I still love You and know Your ways
I certainly hope that I'm able
Day by day You show me Your grace
Your Love ever true and stable

Teach me Your ways and help me learn
All that You've planned for me
Trusting You moment by moment
Unveil my eyes, help me see

I tend to be short sighted
You have so much more in store
Stretch my faith as I trust in You
And help me to love You more.

Rebecca A. Keefe
November 12, 2013

<u>Lord, You Are So Worthy</u>

While driving in my car I was just humming and thinking about the goodness of God and how He is so worthy to be praised when I wrote this poem/chorus. Emphasizing that He is all these things to me, I marvel in the fact that He loves me and loves you! It is a chorus but also a poem of praise. When you close yourself away it doesn't have to be in a special room or church. It can simply be in your car, on your walk, as you ride your bike. Yes, still pay attention to your surroundings, but let your mind go quiet. Forget about the bills that need to be paid. Forget about the job for now. Just focus on how great God is. He is truly worthy to be praised. As I was driving in the car all by myself I began to sing this quietly to the Lord: focusing on Him and not on the doctor's appointment I had just come from. It changed how I felt the rest of the day. Let me encourage you today. Whisper Jesus. Recognize that He loves you and as you praise Him, you will be lifted out of yourself into a new appreciation of who God is. He is so worthy to be praised. As you whisper His name, He may whisper back to you!

I Chronicles 16:25 (NLT)

Great is the LORD! He is most worthy of praise! He is to be revered above all gods.

Lord, You Are So Worthy

Lord, you are so worthy
So beautiful, so sweet
Sweet Jesus you're so worthy
As we sit and learn at Your feet

Whisper Jesus

Precious Savior, You're so worthy
So gracious, so wondrous, so true
Master, You're so worthy
My Friend who carries me through
Lord, You are so worthy
So faithful, so true to the end
Lord, You are so worthy
Truly my Forever Friend
Lord, You are so worthy
Your love surrounds me day by day
Lord, You are so worthy
As You teach me how to pray
Lord, You are so worthy
I praise You, O Ancient of days
Lord, You are so worthy
And now I give You praise
Lord You are Worthy
Yes! You are worthy
Lord You are Worthy
Worthy of all our praise
Worthy of all our praise.

In Jesus Name – Amen

Rebecca A. Keefe
August 15, 2013

Love Revealed

Love Revealed was the theme of our annual Ladies Retreat. I was asked to write a poem with that theme and this is how this poem was born. I am amazed constantly of our Savior's great love for me and you. It goes beyond description! If you are a mother, you cannot believe how much love flows from your heart when you hold your newborn baby in your arms for the first time. The labor pains are forgotten immediately! It is a natural flow of your love to your infant. You now possess a self-sacrificing love that you never knew existed. How could this be? It's a natural flow of love. So it is with God only to a greater and more powerful extent. He loves me! He loves you! He gave His son for my sins. For your sins! I can't fathom it or understand it. But, I can accept it and praise Him because He calls me His child. Hallelujah! What a great love that is revealed for you and me! So I Whisper Jesus and thank Him that He revealed His love for me through Jesus Christ our Lord.

I John 3:1 (NLT)

See how very much our heavenly Father loves us, for he allows us to be called his children, and we really are!

Love Revealed

When a Mama births her baby
Her love is as natural as can be
And God who gave His Son for us
Gave freely – His love to you and me

Whisper Jesus

How amazing, the wonder of it all
That He chose me to love
Gave me access to the family of God
I never had to push or shove

He lets me call Him, Father
What joy! What wonderful bliss!
That He would call me His very own
What marvelous love is this!

Thank you Father for this Love Revealed
That extends beyond thought and time
You gave so freely to us all
So I can call You mine.

Love Revealed, not hidden from view
But given for all to receive
NOW we can give our hearts to You
Accepting Your love and believe

I can't seem to quite fathom
The depth of your love for us all
But I can respond to Your Love Revealed
As I answer to Your call.

Rebecca A. Keefe
May 5, 2012

MOSAIC

My good friend, Rev. Denise Ridley of Water's Edge ministry, as well as radio show host, retreat speaker, teacher, minister, and a member of our Women's Ministry team asked me to write a poem about MOSAIC. It is an illustration she uses in her retreats when she speaks. She also used this illustration for our Bethany Ladies Retreat when she was called upon to speak because our featured speaker had to leave early because of inclement weather. So I sat down and began to write this poem dedicated to her ministry. Here it is:

MOSAIC

My Mess is Overcome by the Son of God
who Always Initiates Creative Restoration

M – My mess – like shattered pieces
All scattered on the ground
Just like Humpty Dumpty's shell
Lay splattered – no longer round

O – Overcome by guilt and sorrow
How can I survive the awful break
Yet Overcome by my Savior's goodness
As He begins a new pattern to make

S – Son of God, who was broken and maimed
Hanging on that nasty old tree
Son of God as He rose again
Broken bodies are now set free

Whisper Jesus

A - Always, unending, and forever
He stands ready to give His love
Always, steadfast, enduring
He showers blessings from above

I – Initiates, motivates and directing
As I journey on this way
Initiating His plan and will for my life
As I listen to what He will say

C – Creative Restoration!
Why am I so surprised by His Plan?
He's had it designed and figured out
Since before the world began

He takes my poor shattered pieces
Picks them up and lays them down
He rearranges the sharp edged ones
Sands them smooth and makes them round

He fits in all the right colors
Making a pattern of my broken life
He's taken the anger and guilt away
And removed the tension and strife

What a beautiful Mosaic
He's creative with His love in me
My sins are gone I've been reborn
And at last, my spirit's set free

Whisper Jesus

Broken lives and shattered pieces
You make beautiful in Your sight
Thank you Lord for Your tender Love
For giving me Peace in place of the night

Beauty for ashes You promised
A life fulfilled – set on the right course
Broken pieces to make a Mosaic
New songs instead of remorse.

Rebecca A. Keefe
November 5, 2012

Never Again

As we read the Book of Revelation we are again reminded of the wonderful hope we have in Christ Jesus our Lord, the promise of no more pain, sorrow or death, the reward that Christ has prepared for us. We forget from time to time what a powerful and awesome God we serve. It is hard to imagine a world without turmoil and where peace reigns supreme. I love this following scripture in Revelation 21. It is what prompted this poem: Never Again. What a wonderful picture of God's supreme love! It's where we will not only Whisper Jesus as we bow before him, but also shout His praises. Think of it – Never Again!

Revelation 21:4 (NKJV)

"And God will wipe away every tear from their eyes; there shall be no more death, nor sorrow, nor crying. There shall be no more pain, for the former things have passed away."

Never Again

Today I'm thinking of heaven
And what a Hope we have in Him
How He'll wipe the tears and sorrow away
He'll say to us Never Again!

I can't quite imagine
No more trouble or strife
It's all I've become used to
It's what defines my life

Whisper Jesus

Never again to have pain
Or to see our loved ones die
Never again to have pain and sickness
And never again to sigh

Oh! What a wonderful promise
We have in His divine Word
He tackles all of our enemies
With the power of His mighty Sword

Clothed in His brilliance
For all men to see
Sickness, sadness and sorrow
Will have no choice but to flee!

Today we live by faith
For that wonderful day
When our hearts will be healed
And we hear Him say
"Never Again"

Rebecca A. Keefe
December 4, 2012

New Covenant in Christ Jesus

There are so many theologians, teachers and writers who have written volumes on the study of covenants. We could spend an entire year just studying about them and how to apply the truth covenants portray in our lives. As our group of women attempted to study about the covenants in the Old and New Testament we began to see just how all the covenants pointed to the new covenant in Christ Jesus. We saw how a covenant or an oath was not to be taken lightly. How it is a lasting, binding agreement, one that is honored forever. We saw also how that covenant affects not only the parties who entered into that agreement and oath, but how it directly affects their families as well, a serious binding oath or agreement. We caught a glimpse of the everlasting love of God in all He does, has done, and will do. Sometimes all we could say was "Wow!" When vocabulary fails me sometimes and a truth finally dawns on me, all I can say in amazement is "Wow! In our study we have seen how the message of salvation has been laid out for us from Genesis to Revelation. How God wants us to be free! From our sin, from our sorrow, from our shame and from our past!

"Thank you Jesus that You have done just that! Grant us the faith to believe fully in Your promises! Thank you Lord that I can simply Whisper "Jesus" and you are here in my midst. You are always here. Thank you for the freedom we have in You."

John 8:36 (NLT)

So if the Son makes you free, you will be free indeed.

Whisper Jesus

New Covenant in Christ Jesus

How blessed we are that God loves us
And made a way of escape from our sin
We are no longer condemned or lost
When we ask Christ to dwell within

Covenants from Abraham to David
New covenant through Christ our Lord
To those who were in the Upper Room
All gathered in one accord

To us right here in this present day
Forgiveness of sin is free
All we need to do is ask
Sweet Jesus – Please forgive me!

Salvation so rich and sweet
The Holy Spirit to infill our being
The New Covenant in Christ is ours
No longer blind but now, seeing

Perhaps you've never known Him
Who takes all guilt and sin away
Let me introduce you to Jesus
Who wants to come into your heart to stay

Forgiveness of sin and despair
From guilt and sorrow set free
"If the Son sets you free
you are free, yes free indeed"

Whisper Jesus

Ask Jesus to come into your heart
You will experience joy beyond measure
You'll find a new freedom from your guilt
And experience a Love you will treasure

Covenants old and new in Christ
Promises of God – forever
His love is everlasting, sure and solid
And He will leave me – never!

Thank You Sweet Lord
That You died for me!

Rebecca A. Keefe
February 25, 2014

<u>No Fishing Allowed</u>

As we grow older we become forgetful at times. Or when things like life gets hectic and busy, we can become forgetful. Yet, there are times when we are not so forgetful. We tend to remember the mistakes we have made, as well as the sins we have committed and have humbly repented of. Those things we have truly asked God to forgive us of - He no longer remembers against us. The scripture says He will cast them into the depths of the sea. The devil, on the other hand, would like to accuse us and cause us to go fishing in the sea where our sins have been cast. This is when we have the liberty, authority and privilege of posting a "No Fishing Allowed" sign. God has forgiven me, washed my sins away and that settles it, thank you God. You are so good! He has removed my sins - never to be remembered against me again. How precious is that?! So if you are fishing in those forbidden waters, get off that fishing boat and go rest in the arms of our precious Savior and Lord. Lean on His breast and softly Whisper Jesus.

Micah 7:19 (NKJV)

He will have compassion on us and subdue our iniquities. You will cast our sins into the depths of the sea.

No Fishing Allowed

The Sea of God's Forgetfulness
It's waters are wide and deep
It's where my sins are cast away
It's a place where I no longer weep

Whisper Jesus

When pressed into a wall of worry
I start fishing over things I have done
No fishing allowed His Spirit says
The battle's not yours and it's won

I'm coming again to take you Home
Where all worries and cares will cease
I'm with you now in the place you're in
My power will never decrease

The battle is Mine, God's says in His Word
And the battles you face He will fight
No fishing allowed in the things of the past
As you trust in His Love and might.

Micah 7:19 (NLT)
…. You will cast all our sins
into the depths of the sea.

Rebecca A. Keefe
October 23, 2012

Not Worthy But Grateful

Studying the characters of the Bible gives us such a unique picture of their strengths and weaknesses. God used ordinary men to accomplish great things for His kingdom. This should be an encouragement for you and me. If God uses ordinary men and women, then if we are willing, He can use us too! Especially men like the apostle Paul who tried to wipe out the Christians of his day before he found Christ Jesus for himself. Or rather, Christ found him! That changed everything. So it is with us. Coming to Jesus changes everything! We are not worthy, but we are oh so grateful! He came for me and he came for you! Have you thought about Jesus today? When is the last time you quieted you and simply whispered the Name of Jesus inviting Him into your life and heart? When you whisper Jesus – the result is that He calms your heart. He causes you to take time and just breathe. Try it today. Whisper "Jesus".

I Timothy 1:12-17 (NLT)

How thankful I am to Christ Jesus our Lord for considering me trustworthy and appointing me to serve him.
even though I used to scoff at the name of Christ. I hunted down his people, harming them in every way I could. But God had mercy on me because I did it in ignorance and unbelief.
Oh how kind and gracious the Lord was! He filled me completely with faith and the love of Christ Jesus.
This is a true saying, and everyone should believe it: Christ Jesus came into the world to save sinners – and I was the worst of them all.
But that is why God had mercy on me, so that Christ Jesus could use me as a prime example of his great patience with the worst of

sinners. Then others will realize that they, too, can believe in him and receive eternal life.

Glory and honor to God forever and ever. He is the eternal King, the unseen one who never dies; He alone is God. Amen.

Not Worthy but Grateful

Jesus paid a price I am not worthy of
But I am so grateful that He did
To take my sin upon Himself
After I committed all He had forbid

He changed and transformed my foolish life
Showed me His patience, mercy and grace
He showed me His love is amazing
As He folds me into His embrace

That means if He died for me
He will strengthen me day after day
He'll show me if I am right or wrong
He will send help, when needed, my way

He gives me examples in His Word
Of saints who have gone before
Abraham, Isaac, Jacob, & Job
Daniel, David, Isaiah and more

So many prophets who listened to God
Twelve disciples who followed our Lord
He sanctified, justified and anointed them
Keeping them all in one accord

Whisper Jesus

Would my Savior die for me
And not strengthen me for each test
No, if He calls me, He'll equip me
He'll give me wisdom and give me rest

He has a plan for my life and yours
He knows you and me by name
He's placed His love within our hearts
As a result we are never the same

You are the Great Example
How You save, justify and position
How You sanctify and clean us up
And show us each Your mission

Help us Lord to hear Your voice
We're not worthy but oh so grateful
Help us spread the Good News far and wide
And most of all – be found faithful

Make it so, Lord Jesus

Rebecca A. Keefe
October 1, 2013

<u>O Lord Be With Us Today</u>

O Lord Be with Us Today was written in 1967 when I was a young mom looking out the window at the busy neighborhood we lived in, watching the children play and people in motion. Everyone was going along doing their own thing. Life seemed to be so normal. To look on the surface it seemed no one had any problems. Yet, we know that is not true.

I was reminded of this poem/song/prayer I wrote many years ago as I watched the bombing of the Boston Marathon and the prayer in my heart is "O Lord Heal Our Land!"

Rebecca A. Keefe
April 16, 2013

O Lord be With us Today

A song I wrote in 1967:

As I look at the people
As they hurry on their way
Taking time with their children
Taking time for work and play
Taking time for everything
As they hurry on their way
Yet no time is left for Jesus
And no time is left to pray

Chorus
O Lord Be With Us Today

Whisper Jesus

As we go our way
Walk beside us
Each step of the way
Go Before us
Go Behind us
Walk Beside us, I pray
O Lord Be With Us
For we need you today

Lord, help me not to be a robot
Help me feel, and let me see
All the many needs of others
Let me, an encouragement be
Help me be aware of darkness
That abounds on every hand
Help me point the Way to Jesus
Lead me by the Master's Hand

Chorus
O Lord Be With Us Today
As we go our way
Walk beside us
Each step of the way
Go Before us
Go Behind us
Walk Beside us, I pray
O Lord Be With Us
For we need you today

Rebecca A. Keefe
Originally written in 1967

<u>Our Thoughts vs His Thoughts</u>

In reading the Old Testament book of Malachi we see again the Israelites facing a broken homeland. They cry out to God. He hears their prayer once again. Even though there are those in Israel who refuse God's way, there are still remnants who call on His Name and He hears their prayer. We may think God doesn't care anymore, but that is simply not true. When His people called on Him he listened and He gave them a promise of redemption. They needed a reminder to turn back to God. If we need to get back on track, and set things right in the eyes of the Lord, it is hard work. Not glamorous work, but necessary work to rebuild. As the poem says simply this is my prayer "thoughting". This is another reason it is so beneficial to read the stories in the Bible of saints who have gone before us. It is so encouraging to see how God moved in their midst. If He could do it then, He can do it now. Like the scripture says - Yesterday, today, forever, Jesus is the same.

Malachi 4:1-2) (NLT)

"The day of judgment is coming, burning like a furnace. The arrogant and the wicked will be burned up like straw on that day. They will consumed like a tree – roots and all.
But for you who fear my name, the Son of righteousness will rise with healing in his wings. And you will go free, leaping with joy like calves let out to pasture."

Our Thoughts vs His Thoughts

Like the Israelites in Malachi's day who neglected God were
reminded

of who they where they were and where they needed to be in God's
eyes.
my prayer thoughting.....

Your Promise is true
But it's not as I thought
It's just not the same
As a favorite toy bought

I thought it was better
Much brighter with more flare
Instead it's hard work
As my strength is laid bare

I know where I'm at
Indeed in Your Divine will
But it's far less glamorous
Thinking it would have more thrill

So what's the next step?
Show me where the pieces go
Help me hear Your voice in trouble
Listening to the One I know

I have simply no desire
To turn completely back now
I need Your direction
Your Spirit showing me how

My thoughts get so scattered

Whisper Jesus

Your thoughts high and secure
I can lose focus so easily
Yet Your Word does endure

So keep me Lord from failing,
Doing what I think best
Doing Your will only
Never failing Your test.

By Your Grace Lord

Rebecca A. Keefe
May 21, 2013

Palms Up!

It is so good to have steady reminders in family and friends. Reminders that we need to give up whatever we are struggling with to Jesus. A while back I was fussing about something and talking to my daughter Debby when she said to me, "Palms up Mom, Give it to Jesus!" It was a repeat of what I had said to her earlier." I just need to lift my hands up to Jesus – Palms Up – and give it to Him." She was right! I can be wringing my hands, worrying or fussing and fuming about something or someone, when all I need to do a "Palms Up" to Jesus. "Here it is Lord, You take care of it." That's when He comes in and restores peace to my troubled heart. Old hurts sometimes surface, hard memories pop up every now and then. Situations that were troubling that I thought had been forgotten when a glimmer of the pain returns. I forget sometimes that all I need to do is lift my hands upward, palms up and simply say "Not going there Lord, it's Yours to handle." It's so much easier that way! First, I need to quiet myself – stop – and perhaps softly whisper the Name of Jesus. Change my focus from me to Him. It works every time! It's a choice. I can cry and moan and complain, or I can lift it up to Jesus.

I Peter 5:7 (NIV)

Cast all your anxieties on him because he cares for you.

I Peter 5:7 (NLT)

Give all your worries and cares to God, for he cares about you.

Whisper Jesus

Palms up!

How do I hold this up to You
When what happened blows me away?
How do I even stand up straight?
When it's all I can do to stay?

Past – Present – Future
I lift them up to You just now.
I'm not sure how I can handle this
But, I am sure You'll show me how!

Casting all my cares on You
That's what the scriptures say
I am not equipped to handle the pain
But You have taught me to pray!

Palms Up – I hand it up to You
It's too much for me to bear.
Palms Up – You do the work
And all my worries share!

Thank you Jesus!

Rebecca A. Keefe
October 2, 2012

<u>Prayers – vs – Pray-ers</u>

When we talk about prayer we must also talk about the one who offers a prayer – the pray-er. There are times when we pray out of desperation – wanting God to move quickly and other times it can be a prayer offered in praise. Nonetheless, however and whenever we pray we have to believe that God exists and that he is a rewarder of those who seek His face. The scripture clearly states that faith is involved when we pray. It is a time to examine our motives. Why am I praying? What do I hope will be the eventual outcome? Do I believe that God is really there to hear to hear my plea? Personally, if I could not come to God in prayer I would be a woman most desperate, and without hope. He is my Peace, my Comfort, and My Friend. I truly want to be a dedicated Pray-er, one who comes to God with a pure heart but I cannot do that without His Spirit abiding in me, guiding me as I pray. Simply and quietly whispering Jesus, knowing He hears me and is right here beside me.

Hebrews 11:1 (NLT)

What is faith? It is the confident assurance that what we hope for is going to happen. It is the evidence of things we cannot yet see.

Hebrews 11:1 (KJV)

Now faith is the substance of things hoped for, the evidence of things not seen.

Hebrews 11:6 (NIV)

And without faith it is impossible to please God, because anyone who comes to him must believe that he exists and that he rewards those who earnestly seek him.

Ephesians 3:12 (NIV)

In him and through faith in him we may approach God with freedom and confidence

I John 5:13-15 (NIV)

I write these things to you who believe in the name of the Son of God so that you may know that you have eternal life. This is the confidence we have in approaching God; that if we ask anything to his will, he hears us. And if we know that he hears us – whatever we ask – we know that we have what we asked of him.

Prayers – vs – Pray-ers

I know that prayers make a difference
Coming to God with a heart that's sincere
When my mind is in meditation
As I ask Him to please draw near

And I know when I am the pray-er
Reaching out to God in prayer
My hardened heart is changed forever
As I bring my burdens to share

Whisper Jesus

But sometimes the prayer is selfish
It's all about me and mine, and myself
It's about things I'd like to have right now
Not a thing to be put on the shelf

At times I whine trying to control the Lord
As I choose my words in my prayer
Or I try to persuade Him I am worthy
That I should be treated fair

Do I just pray a memorized prayer?
Which is beautiful in and of itself
Yet the Master bids me come to Him
So I can learn still more of Himself

Do you God, make mistakes like common man
Do you really know my name?
When life doesn't make any sense at all
Can I trust that prayer is not a game?

The answer is truly simple
For I believe God has a plan for my life
He's promised to go with me
And deliver me from all kinds of strife

Delight myself in Him wholly
Giving praise to the Father above
With words from my heart sincerely
Thanking Him for His wonderful love

Your Word is founded on truth and love

Whisper Jesus

On the fact that it is solid and sure
You ask that I trust and simply believe
And You'll show me Your Love will endure

Lord help me not to just say nice prayers
But help me a Pray-er be
To have a heart of compassion
To feel the heart of those in need

Most of all dear Jesus
I give you praise for all that You have done
For your great sacrifice on Calvary
And all the victories You have won

Thank You for the Word of God
Which teaches me how to pray
And as I try to be a Pray-er
I know You will teach what to say.

Make it so Lord Jesus

Rebecca A. Keefe
June 10, 2014

Puzzle Piece

How are you with puzzles? Me? Not so good. If it is a child's puzzle, no problem, I can see the big pieces and it's a fun exercise. But give me a big puzzle with a thousand pieces and watch me go bonkers. I might even consider cutting a piece to fit. It is just not my thing! In our lives there are times when all the pieces seem to fit perfectly. Life is good. No problems. We sigh and relax. Then one of those puzzle pieces gets booted out of place by an unexpected disruption and now everything is out of balance. There is a plan to the puzzle, and sometimes, the more we look at the puzzle one of two things can happen. We see the pattern and have an "ah ha" moment where we get just a glimpse of the big picture or it becomes a big blur. We must constantly go back and look at the box cover for the example of what the final puzzle picture is all about and search for that missing piece to make the puzzle complete. Not so much different in our walk with the Lord is it? Sometimes all the pieces seem to fit perfect, and then we go through a period where we lose sight of the example and we need to go back and look at the original. The Bible, God's Word. When we do that – then we can see He has a plan where all those pieces will come together again. They fit perfectly like they were designed to and we didn't have to cut any pieces to fit according to our design. It's His design that makes it all come together. And let me say it again. Whisper Jesus. He is the great example. He is the one who makes all the puzzle pieces fit together.

Jeremiah 29:11-13 (NLT)

"For I know the plans I have for you," says the LORD. "They are plans for good and not disaster, to give you a future and a hope.

In those days when you pray, I will listen.
If you look for me in earnest, you will find me when you seek me."

Puzzle Piece

Life seems so like a puzzle,
Many pieces of different size.
One day is filled with laughter,
Another day filled with cries

The piece I hold seems to fit in place
I leap for joy and am glad.
When it doesn't fit the puzzle
My frustration turns to mad!

The puzzle looked so perfect,
It looked like it all should fit.
I twisted and turned the puzzle piece
Forged ahead when I should have quit!

I look back now, I should have stopped
I really thought I knew best
I forgot I have an enemy
Who delights when I fail the test!

I'm sorry Lord, I forged ahead
Forgot to ask You to lead
You know where all the pieces fit
It's on Your Grace I plead.

Life is a puzzle, yes that is true

Whisper Jesus

Each piece a part of Your plan
Healing is one piece at a time
Restoration is in Your hand

So once again I yield to You
As You lead me to the right place
The pieces will all fit together now
As I lean on Your Mercy and Grace.

Rebecca A. Keefe
December 12, 2011

Recounting

I believe we all have good "forgetters." We live so much in the moment. My husband relates a story of a woman who used to be a regular customer in the Keefe Brothers Texaco Station he and his father owned in Waltham, Massachusetts. They did many things for this particular customer and when she would come in with another demand, they would try to explain to her allowances they had made for her in the past. Her response was always: "Yes, but what have you done for me lately?" She didn't want to talk about the past or even appreciate what had already been done out of the ordinary service she was rendered. Isn't that a lot like us? In this story of Nehemiah 10, the nation of Israel began to recount all that God had done for them and appreciate His great provision for them and His love. They weren't saying "But what have You done for us lately." As they heard all that God had done for them, they agreed to obey God. Over and over the words we promise are recorded. When we come to God wholeheartedly, God does above and beyond what we could ever ask or think. But here is the bottom line, there is action required on our part. As you read the story of Nehemiah, you become keenly aware that there is a two way interaction going on. Recounting what God has done is so beneficial as well as recounting our heart's dedication to Him. Not forgetting what He has done and what He has promised to do for those who remain faithful. In simply whispering the sweet and powerful Name of Jesus, we can calm our hearts enough to remember His goodness and His faithfulness. Whispering Jesus - Thank You!

Nehemiah 10:28, 29, 30, 32, 35, 38 (NLT)

The rest of the people-the priests, Levites, gatekeepers, singers, Temple servants, and all who had separated themselves from the pagan people of the land in order to serve God, and who were old enough to understand - now all heartily bound themselves with an oath. They vowed to accept the curse of God if they failed to obey the law of God issued by his servant Moses. They solemnly promised to carefully follow all the commands, laws, and regulations of the LORD their Lord.

So we promise....

In addition, we promise....

We promise always ....

....."So we promise together not to neglect the Temple of our God."

Recounting

The Israelites looked back
Recounting all that God had done
How they'd fought so many battles
The countless victories they had won

Recounting when they were following God
And when they were doing wrong
Recounting how when they were slaves
They indeed had lost their song

They saw God's mighty hand deliver
They saw His mercy and His grace
They saw how He was still with them
When they'd fallen in disgrace

Whisper Jesus

Yet when they called upon His name
Recounting and confessing their sin
They saw firsthand how quick He came
To help them begin again

Thank you God for the Israelites
And prophets of ages past
Who confessed their sins as they came to You
How you gave them peace that would last

You caused rivers to flow in the desert
You caused waters and seas to part
You caused great kings to repent
As Your word to them you'd impart

Help me Lord to recount and remember
All the ways You've shown me Your love
The battles fought and victories won
Through Your Mercy and Grace from above

When I read about the others
Your precious Word talks about
It gives me pause to wonder
It makes me want to shout!

Thank You Jesus!

Rebecca A. Keefe
June 5, 2012

REDEEMED

Redeemed was the theme for our annual fall retreat for the ladies of Bethany Assembly of God in Agawam, Massachusetts. I was asked to write a poem to go along with that theme. Thus, this poem was born. When we read the book of Ruth, we learn about a kinsman redeemer, someone who has the power to redeem, rescue and restore. This is a beautiful story and example of the great love of our kinsman redeemer, Jesus Christ. He redeems. He rescues. He restores. How wonderful that we have been redeemed. God's redemptive work has far reaching unbelievable results. Ruth was redeemed by Boaz; they had a son named Obed. Obed was the father of Jesse and Jesse was the father of David. And David is in the lineage of Christ. Wow! God redeems us not because of anything we have done, but because of His great love. Thank you Jesus! He loves me and you with an everlasting love. He doesn't give up on us as easily as we give up on one another. He cares enough for us to redeem us! Think about it. I will never understand the depths of His love. But I accept it! Again, thank you Jesus! Let me encourage you to simply whisper "Jesus" with a thankful heart. He looked beyond my sin, as a songwriter once put it, and saw my need, my need of a redeemer.

REDEEMED

Isaiah 43:1 NIV
"For I have redeemed you; I have summoned
you by name; you are mine."

When I think that the God of the universe

Whisper Jesus

Made provision that I be redeemed
I am amazed and astonished at His love
When all I could do was blaspheme

I find it hard to understand and fathom
That He has summoned me by my name
That He paid the price forward for my sin
When I was guilty and carried all blame

Jesus came to win back what was stolen
On the Cross so long long ago
Taking deceit and foolishness
Redeeming the lies that were sown

He made good and atoned for all
My mistakes and my foolish pride
He covered my sins with His sacrifice
And made me His chosen Bride

Though unworthy, broken and guilty
He loves me as His very own
He's redeemed my life with his own blood
And healed all my broken bones

He bought me back when a slave of sin
Wrote my name in the palm of His hand
No longer bound but free indeed
He brought me to His promised land

Redeemed and set free no longer bound
Bought with a price beyond measure

Whisper Jesus

Redeemed, Restored and Repaired
Redeemed I've become His treasure

Redeemed How I Love to Proclaim It
Is a song of praise we sing
I'll love Him forever, I'll love Him now
And forever His Praises I'll bring

REDEEMED!

Rebecca A. Keefe
October 2013

Bethany Assembly of God
Agawam, Massachusetts
Women's Fall Retreat

Reflect – Remember – Repent

The Lord's Supper or Communion is the perfect time to reflect, remember and repent. This affords us the opportunity to stop for a moment and not rush. It is a time to perhaps whisper "Jesus" as the name of this book suggests. Sitting in a meditative state of mind, letting all else go by the wayside, just whisper the sweet Name of Jesus. It will change you! He will change you as you invite Him to come along beside you and dwell within your heart. This is truly the new covenant we have in Christ Jesus. We as gentiles have been grafted into the divine Vine. We can now be called the children of God. We are so blessed and privileged. Let me invite you to whisper "Jesus" the very next time you take communion or participate in the Lord's Supper. You will not be disappointed.

I Corinthians 11:23-32 (NASB)

For I received from the Lord that which I also delivered to you, that the Lord Jesus on the night in which He was betrayed took bread; and when He had given thanks, He broke it and said, "This is My body, which is for you; do this in remembrance of Me. "In the same way He took the cup also after supper, saying, "This cup is the new covenant in My blood; do this, as often as you drink it, in remembrance of Me." For as often as you eat this bread and drink the cup, you proclaim the Lord's death until He comes. Therefore whoever eats the bread or drinks the cup of the Lord in an unworthy manner shall be guilty of the body and the blood of the Lord. But a man must examine himself, and in so doing he is to eat of the bread and drink of the cup. For he who eats and drinks, eats and drinks judgment to him if he does not judge the body rightly. For this reason many among you are weak and sick, and a number sleep.

But if we judged ourselves rightly, we would not be judged. But when we are judged, we are disciplined by the Lord so that we will not be condemned along with the world.

Reflect – Remember – Repent

Looking at the word Covenant
In God's Word both old and new
I am astounded by its meaning
Which is sacred, binding and true

As we partake of The Lord's Supper
Celebrating the New Covenant in His Blood
We reflect on past covenants
That started with Noah and the flood

We remember how binding is this oath
Sworn by our Father above
Repenting of all our foolish sins
As we accept Jesus through His blood

A binding, solemn agreement
That is sealed for all eternity
I take on His cloak of righteousness
As He takes on my humanity

I re-dedicate my heart to Him
Submitting myself to Him alone

Whisper Jesus

I thank Him for His great sacrifice
And for all my sins He atoned

The broken bread symbolizes His body
Which was broken and beaten for me
The wine which is a reminder
That His shed blood sets me free

I rejoice because He loves me so
Giving his life on Calvary
Though unworthy, sinful and lost
Because of Him I have victory

The covenants in the Old Testament
Serious and binding, holding fast
The New Covenant in Christ Jesus
Holds for eternity that will forever last

So as I Reflect, Remember and Repent
I will Return, Rededicate and Rejoice
God's only Son took on my sin
Being willing to be God's choice

Help us Lord to always remember
Your New Covenant is binding and true
Help us live our lives in a pleasing manner
That will always bring Glory to You!

Make it so Lord Jesus!

Rebecca A. Keefe

January 28, 2014

Rise Up and Believe!

Have you ever wept hard tears of remorse over things that have happened in the past, over things that you have done? You may not have realized how wrong you were or how far down the wrong path you had gone? It was like this in the Book of Nehemiah. Ezra the prophet read the Law to the people and they wept bitterly. After they heard the words of Ezra, they repented and once again returned to the LORD. Then Ezra encouraged them to rise up and believe. Don't be dejected or sad for the joy of the Lord is your strength. We live in difficult times, a world at war on every front. It is scary out there! We also can turn from God and go down a different path than the one He has planned for us. It is never too late to repent and return and rise up and believe. Let me encourage you today. Rise up and believe that God is real. God is everywhere present. God is all powerful and He knows you by name. Come to Him today and believe. You will find as this scripture says: The joy of the Lord is your strength and strength comes by spending time in His presence, in a quiet place, perhaps simply a place where you can Whisper "Jesus." Rise up today and do just that.

Nehemiah 8:10 (NLT)

Don't be dejected or sad for the joy of the Lord is your strength.

Rise Up and Believe!

Living in the power of the Lord
In the middle of difficult times

Whisper Jesus

How does that really work out
In my life as each hour chimes?

I was born with a nature to worry
Contrary to trust and believe
I go to worry and fretting first
Before I, His love, receive

The choice is ever before me
Believe God can do all things
Or choose doubt and disappointment
Or Rise Up like on angels wings

I belong to God Almighty
On His palm my name is written
The victory is mine for the asking
And my foe is already smitten

Faith will grow in my heart and soul
As I come to Him in prayer
I can Rise Up and believe in Him
Or I can live my life in despair

The Joy of the Lord is truly my strength
As I place my trust in You
You show me there's no valley so low
That You grace can't bring me through

Help me Sweet Lord to remember
Should I start to worry through the day
That all I really need to do is

Whisper Jesus

Rise Up! Believe You! And Pray!

You promised Joy for the Journey
I don't have to carry this burden alone
You said You'd never leave nor forsake me
As I place my needs at Your throne

So I rest my weary soul in You
Knowing You do all things well
You give mercy, grace, joy and strength
As my storms You'll always quell

Thank You Sweet Jesus!

Rebecca A. Keefe
April 8, 2014

<u>Secrets</u>

Secrets, we all have them. Secrets are just that – something we want to keep hidden or not spoken out loud. Sometimes secrets are dark, rarely spoken about. Yet, God sees us even in a dark place, in the here and now as well as in the past. This is the amazing part of salvation. Our secrets, our sins, confessed to Him, are removed from us as far as the East is from the West. Never to be remembered against us. God wipes the slate clean. He gives us a brand new heart. Isn't that amazing?!

"Here again Lord, we see that You offer each one of us so much! Friendship with You is like no other. You love us as we are. You come into our hearts and lives and show us there is more to life than merely existing. You show us that friendship with You is a joy. You never disappoint us or fail us.

You stay with us even when we may try to hide things from You. Yet, You keep all that we commit to You, and You forgive us and set us on the right path. Most of all Jesus, Your love never fails. How blessed we are! Thank You Lord!"

Psalm 25:14 (NLT)

Friendship with the LORD is reserved for those who fear him. With him he shares the secrets of his covenant.

Psalm 103:11-12 (NIV)

For as high as the heavens are above the earth, so great is his love for those who fear him;
as far as the east is from the west, so far has he removed our transgressions from us.

2 Timothy 1:12 (NLT)

…...for I know whom I have believed, and persuaded that he is able to keep that which I committed to him against that day.

Secrets

I thank you Lord for Your keeping power
All that I committed to You is covered
I've gone from being Your enemy
To becoming Your precious beloved

Just like the calling placed within my heart
By Your Holy Spirit divine
Is committed to You in this same way
As the work is Yours and not mine

We hold secrets deep within ourselves
Some dark with hurt and despair
But You erase all the despondency
As we enter our closet of prayer

Those things we commit to You in prayer
The ugly, the good, the bad
You sort them out by Your divine love
As You make our broken hearts glad

Whisper Jesus

Secrets we thought hidden – brought to light
In our time spent with you alone
Your Sea of Forgetfulness covers them all
They're no longer ours to own

We not only commit to You our sins but
The work You've called us to do
Secrets revealed in your great light
Sins forgiven then called to work for You

Holding these things deep in our heart
Like Mary when visited by Your angel
Waiting for the time to speak Your word
Knowing when to reveal is special

The mountain top shout may have to wait
As we hold dear to our hearts your promise
Experiencing peace and joy and love
And the Holy Spirit calmness

So many examples in Your word
Men and women who remained true
Help us Lord to manifest Your love
And be an example too.

Make it so Lord Jesus

Rebecca A. Keefe
December 10, 2013

<u>Seeds</u>

Planting a garden of vegetables or flowers has always been fun for me. I love to get my hands in the dirt. As a child I can remember my Italian grandfather planting a garden in his backyard in his pristine little neighborhood. My father also loved to plant a garden and my brothers as well. I have a very small garden that abuts my patio and it is fun to see how quickly things grow and the fruit they produce from one tiny little seed. I also see how quickly the weeds want to strangle anything that is planted and how diligence is needed to keep my little garden productive. I gave the Bethany Ladies Bible Study a packet of seeds that symbolized the seed of God's Word. Every time I look at a new packet of seeds I am reminded of this verse. Are we fertile ground for the Holy Spirit to work in or do we have rocky soil in our spirit that would prevent Him moving in our hearts? Stop for a moment and think about your own little spiritual garden. Is there room for God's Word to grow? Do you water it daily with prayer? Is there danger of the seed being strangled by too much busyness? Hmm, I wonder. Maybe I just need to slow down a bit. Perhaps I need to simply sit quietly and whisper "Jesus."

Matthew 13 tells about seed that is planted on four kinds of soil and what happens to it, the hard path, the rocky soil, the thorny ground and the good soil.

Matthew 13:19-23 (NLT)

The seed that fell on the hard path represents those who hear the Good News about the Kingdom and don't understand it. Then the evil one comes and snatches the seed away from their hearts.

The rocky soil represents those who hear the message and receive it with joy.

21/ But like young plants in such soul, their roots don't go very deep. At first they get along fine, but they wilt as soon as they have problems or are persecuted because they believe the word.

The thorny ground represents those who hear and accept the Good News, but all too quickly the message is crowded out by the cares of this life and the lure of wealth, so no crop is produced.

23.. The good soil represents the hearts of those who truly accept God's message and produce a huge harvest – thirty, sixty, or even a hundred times as much as had been planted.

1 Peter 1:23 (NIV)

For you have been born again, not of perishable seed, but of imperishable, through the living and enduring Word of God.

Seeds

Here in my hand is a packet of seeds
I wonder how they'll grow.
How will I plant the tiny pods?
Will I line them up in a row?

What will they need and where will they grow?
What kind of things do they need?
How shall I plant, how long should I wait
to produce a plant from my seed?

Whisper Jesus

Yet, before I reap a harvest,
There's some digging I must do.
Throwing out the rocks and clay
And, plowing till I'm through

Lots of weeds, and thorny things
And stuff to thwart the seed
Yet once it's cleared and ready
I can plant my seeds indeed.

Lord, plant Your Word deep in my heart
and weed out sin and greed.
Plow up my hard and fallow ground
And let me see Your need.

I can do some digging in my soil
But You dig deeper still
My heart needs yielded to Your plow
As You plant in me, Your Will

I want to be the seed You plant
I want my life to grow in You
I give my heart to you today
Do with it what You will.

Please take these seeds we share today
May it bring a smile to Your face
Help us yield our lives to you right now
each day, and in this place.

Amen
Rebecca A. Keefe
May 1, 2011

The Story of the Rubber Band
Snap Back into Focus!

After I retired from Gordon College in Wenham, Massachusetts, I worked part time for 8 years at Weight Watchers. One of the leaders used the illustration of the Rubber Band to help the members refocus. She gave everyone in her meeting a rubber band. Her instructions were to put a rubber band around our wrist for a week. When we became tempted to eat something that was fattening or bad for us just snap that rubber band. The stings of that snap would snap us back into focus. Not a bad illustration for us in a spiritual sense as well. Perhaps we need a reminder to Snap Back into Focus every once in a while. What do you think? Do you need a reminder every once in a while to refocus - or snap back into reality? Have I talked with Jesus today? Have I taken time to simply whisper Jesus or am I too busy? Would it help if I had a visual reminder like this little rubber band that would leave a sting if I snapped it? "Lord help me to stay focused without a snap or a sting! Let it be a natural thing for me to come to You daily and just Whisper Jesus. By Your Grace, Amen"

The Story of the Rubber Band
Snap Back into Focus!

Snap Back Into Focus.
Ouch! That hurt!
Yes that's what I need

Whisper Jesus

Get my mind off me
And back onto Thee.

Snap Back Into Focus.
Ouch! That hurt!
I've done it again
Got out of focus
And whining again.

Snap Back Into Focus.
Ouch! That hurt!
What is that they say?
What's that over there?
Doesn't really matter...
.....I guess I need to pray.

Rebecca A. Keefe
October 2009

<u>Sometimes, Lord</u>

Have you ever struggled to get something to work and no matter what you did or said it just didn't come together? Sometimes it's with people, sometimes its places, sometimes and its things. Have you ever struggled to make a relationship work only to have it fall completely apart? Or apologize and your apology was not accepted? Or perhaps you wanted to take a trip and no matter how well you planned there was always something that prevented it from happening. Then there is applying for a job that you really want. You have the qualifications, you just know you will be selected, but you are not. What's up with that? Sometimes you just don't understand. Perhaps it's a simple problem like your printer and computers are not compatible. Nothing you do fixes the problem. When that happened recently I called my son Cj, who tried to work his computer magic on the problem without success. We spent a lot of time trying to connect the two. Or rather, he spent a lot of time while I watched! Then he suggested that I return the printer since it was obvious that the printer and the computer were just not going to work together. That simple suggestion came after a lot of time and much frustration of trying to make it work!

After wasting a lot of precious time trying to do things on my own, I finally come to the place when I earnestly ask the Lord to show me His direction.

"No matter how hard I pray for it – if it is not Your Will Lord .... Don't give it to me. Because I know in my heart if it is not

Your will then it's not where I should be. So don't listen to my whining. You have Your way."

Is it easy to say that prayer? Oh no! I am a stubborn woman! Or so my kids tell me. I prefer to call it determined and not stubborn. Nevertheless, I truly want God's way, even though I still say, "Sometimes, Lord." And as always, quietly whisper Jesus.

Sometimes, Lord

Sometimes, Lord I just don't know
Which direction I'm supposed to go.

Are my eyes wide open or just squeezed shut tight?
Should I go left or straight or veer to the right?

My heart knows, Lord. Your way is best,
But sometimes Sweet Jesus I fail the test

When I look at the options my way – or Your path
As I add up the cost You have the best math

I can't see the forest because of the trees
Clear away the clutter make Your way plain for me!

Mind, body, soul, so real and so true!
It all works together so I yield it all to You.

Rebecca A. Keefe
September 27, 2011

Stop! Look! Listen!

We get so busy! Time flies by so quickly. If you've ever decided to check your email or Facebook for just a second in the morning I'm sure you can identify. Personally speaking, I've checked things out and it was early, then I got interested in this chat or that article and I look up at the clock and 2 hours has passed. How did that happen? Yet, at the same time I can say I am too busy to sit and pray. Has that ever happened to you? This little poem is just a reminder that time spent with Jesus is never wasted once we finally stop. Just stop. Sit quietly. No outside noise. Just quiet. In a house with six kids and a dog, my mom's quiet place was the bathroom. Yes! The bathroom! No one would disturb her there! You could also walk into her kitchen and see an open Bible on her table. So where is your quiet place? Where is it that you just stop – look – and listen for God to speak to you? Let me invite you to do that right now. Stop. Be quiet. Just Listen. Perhaps Whisper the Name of Jesus softly. Invite the sweet Holy Spirit to come in and calm your heart and soul. Do it. It is time well spent.

Job 37:14 (NIV)

Listen to this Job, stop and consider God's wonders.

Psalm 105:4 (NIV)

Look to the LORD and his strength; seek his face always.

Proverbs 1:5 (NIV)

Let the wise listen and add to their learning

Stop! Look! Listen!

Stop!- Look! – Listen!
Can you hear?
God's still small voice
Whispering in your ear?

Are you quiet enough?
As you scurry around
Are you working so hard?
That you can't hear a sound?

"What? Are You speaking?"
"Speak louder!" you say,
"I've so much to do,
Not enough hours in the day!"

"O Lord, can't you visit
As I rush through each hour?
Must I sit with You
To experience Your power?"

"Come aside." You say
"How can that be?
There's kids, family, work
And no time left for me!"

Whisper Jesus

"Stop – Look – Listen!
It's impossible I say.
But if You insist,
I will do it Your way."

"Okay – so I've stopped
Quiet feels nice in this place.
There's peace in the stillness
As I look on Your face."

"I'm sorry I hurried
And lost sight of You
By Your grace, Lord,
I'll be quiet and listen to You."

Rebecca A. Keefe
October 21, 2011

<u>Stories of Love</u>

If you've never read the book of Hosea, then I invite you to sit down right now and read it. Then read all the footnotes and comments that go along with it. I love the Life Application Bible in any version or translation because it shows us how to simply apply the lessons we read about in scripture. Sometimes we read a scripture and we may think it irrelevant, until we start thinking about it. We wonder how can what we read apply to our everyday life. The book of Hosea is a wonderful example of the Love of God for the unfaithful. This book is so special because it clearly illustrates how God is willing to rescue His loved ones over and over. It shows us how great the love of God truly is. How blessed we are that the love of God is so far reaching and so patient! As we Whisper Jesus in our prayers and interaction with others, we begin to see how far reaching and endless His love is.

Hosea 3:1 (NLT)

"Then the LORD said to me, 'Go and get your wife again. Bring her back to you and love her, even though she loves adultery. For the LORD still loves Israel even though the people have turned to other gods, offering them choice gifts'"

Hosea 14:4 NLT

The LORD says, then I will heal you of your faithlessness, my love knows no bounds. For my anger will be gone forever.

Whisper Jesus

Stories of Love

Great stories of Love
Often go against reason
Showing mercy and grace
In all kinds of seasons

Compassion and forgiveness
that keeps reaching beyond
Limitless – unending
Creating love's strong bond

That's the way God loves me
Beyond my wildest dreams
He casts aside my failings
And all my foolish schemes

He shows me that I'm worthy
That His love will never end
He gives me Joy and Glory
He's my Forever Friend

I truly don't deserve Him
But He died that I might live
His heart now beats in my heart
His love I'll never outlive

Turning from my faithlessness

Whisper Jesus

Confessing all my sin
Allows His love to flow freely
As I turn my life to Him

Thank You God for Your promise
That your anger is turned away
Thank You for Grace and Mercy
And that Your Love is here to stay.

Thank You Jesus!

Rebecca A. Keefe
June 4, 2013

Strength For The Journey

I get bone-tired sometimes. It seems like that tiredness starts from the inside and works its way outward. Sometimes I think the tiredness comes because I'm trying too hard. I think I have to be strong. After going through numerous extensive surgeries I have realized there are limits to what I can physically do! It's like my mind says, "Go! Go!" but my body answers, "No! No!" "Just not going to happen girl. Slow down, stop." I find myself pushing the limits sometimes and then I get that rude awakening again. Not a good thing to do! It's not only physical strength that we need on this journey here on earth; it is the strength of the Lord that we need also hence, the inspiration for this poem. The Bible is full of scripture about strength in the Lord. As I read I am reminded to Whisper Jesus and thank Him for His strength. If I forget, I have a reminder in the scripture. Here are just a few scriptures that refer to God's strength:

Psalm 18:32 (NLT)

God arms me with strength; he has made my way safe.

Psalm 118:14 (NLT)

The LORD is my strength and my song; he has become my victory.

Psalm 138:3 (NLT)

Whisper Jesus

When I pray, you answer; you encourage me by giving me the strength I need.

Strength For The Journey

Life, as we know it, is a journey
With paths winding to and fro
We come to Christ just as we are
As we give Him our sins and woe

Including every sin and sickness
All our wanderings and more
We change direction as we come to Him
As He reveals what He has in store

I think my strength has to come from me
Being strong and brave and true
If I'm good enough and fast enough
There's not a battle I can't get through

It is so easy to lose my focus –
and think Life is all about me –
In my misguided understanding
When in fact, Lord, it's not me but Thee

You call me blessed if I place my trust in You
Promising strength for the journey each day
Not from my strength or power or might
But strength from You as I pray

Help me Lord to center my heart on You

Whisper Jesus

And not on this Journey of mine
Show me strength is there for the asking
Remembering I am totally and wholly Thine

When feeling alone in this journey
I need to remember I belong to You
You've planned my way before the world began
And You promise to see me through

Your Word is strong and endures forever
Your promises are sure and true
No matter where I may find myself
My strength is always in You

The outcome is not my worry
You promise strength as the day is long
The journey belongs to You sweet Lord
And in the night You promise a song

So I rest my weary soul in Thee
Knowing my strength comes from on High
I thank You that I'm a child of God
And I never escape Your eye

Thank You Lord for Your Strength!

Written by: Rebecca A. Keefe
March 25, 2014

The Bus

I wrote this poem for my firstborn daughter Deborah Willette Papalegis. She made the statement: "I need to get off the bus and let God do the driving." Debby is a mover and a doer. When she was a toddler her grandma asked if she should be given something to slow her down. She was busy, busy and busy. It's her personality to be a problem solver. Think of a solution, act on it, do it. In her Christian walk there are times she realizes she just needs to sit in the passenger seat or get off the bus entirely and let God do His thing. In the end it works out better. And she, like me, once we finally turn a situation over to the Lord ask ourselves why we didn't do it sooner! We were at Bethany's first annual Ladies Retreat when she made this statement and it prompted me to write this poem. A retreat is a perfect time also to sit quietly and whisper Jesus as we attempt to draw closer to Him. If you find yourself always in the driver's seat, perhaps this is a good time to Whisper Jesus, asking Him to take the wheel.

Romans 8:28 (NLT)

And we know that God causes everything to work together for the good of those who love God and are called according to his purpose for them

The Bus

It really was a shiny bus
I handled it like a charm

Whisper Jesus

The big wheels yielded to my lead
Never thinking I could lead it to harm

I loved being the driver
Dictating which way to go
I never thought of not being in charge
I decided to go fast or go slow

I looked at all of my charges
My responsibilities in each seat
I had their routes all planned in advance
I never once thought of defeat

Then the voice of the Sweet Holy Spirit
Whispered to the deep of my heart
"Why not let me take the wheel
I'll be with you and never depart"

Let You take control? I can't let go –
I need to drive the bus
I need to tell them where to go
I need to worry and fuss

It's been my way of life
We might not make it to the end
I just have to maneuver a little more
Just drive around one more bend

I'm good at skidding and sliding
Even though I'm weary and worn
Let You drive the bus Lord?

Whisper Jesus

I can trust You – but I admit- I am torn

Okay - I think I'll get off now
And let You take control
I'll let You decide which routes to take
All my charges on You I'll roll

Wow! What a difference in my spirit
I'm not screaming or yelling just now
I like not driving the bus anymore
I sat down and You showed me how.

I'm sure I'll want in the driver's seat
But Sweet Spirit remind me again
That You are the one who directs my path
And with you there's no chagrin

You give peace beyond understanding
You go before, beside and behind
You know the safe routes to travel
If I try to drive – Never mind!

Thank you for giving me counsel
Thank you for driving the bus
For showing me I can trust you
It's not just me but it's US!

Rebecca A. Keefe
November 12, 2012

The Pointer

In the news we see the Democrats blaming the Republicans and the Republicans blaming the Democrats. The President blames the Congress; Congress blames the President and one party or group is against the other. We see lawsuits with the accused and the guilty, the defender and the prosecutor, nation against nation. In our families we say it was our brother or our sister as we try to point the blame away from ourselves. The comedian Flip Wilson coined the famous line in comedy that said: "The devil made me do it!" We laugh about it and think it is funny. Yet it is so easy to point the finger at the fault we see in others and at the same time overlook our own mistakes and guilt. I say 'we' what I mean to say is 'I'. We joke in our family because it is very difficult for me to say "I was wrong." The words just stick in my mouth. I will say "You are right" but somehow it is so hard for me to admit that I was or might be 'w – w – wrong'.

Here again brings up the lesson of an apology. A sincere and heartfelt apology has three parts. Number one: "I am sorry." Number two: "I was wrong." Number three: "Will you forgive me? " No pointing the finger and saying the devil made me do it or it's your fault. Or I did that or that because you made me do it. Simply stated, I am sorry, I was wrong, will you forgive me?

"Lord, help us to be responsible and own what is ours to own and ask you to help us along the way. We need You Lord so much!!" Perhaps if I took time to simply Whisper Jesus, I would not be so apt to point at others. Perhaps I would be more forgiving of others also.

Whisper Jesus

Colossians 3:13-16 (NLT)

You must make allowance for each other's faults and forgive the person who offends you. Remember, the Lord forgave you, so you must forgive others.

And the most important piece of clothing you must wear is love. Love is what binds us all together in perfect harmony.

Let the peace that comes from Christ rule in your hearts. For as members of one body you are all called to live in peace. And always be thankful.

Let the words of Christ, in all their richness, live in your hearts and make you wise.

The Pointer

It's so easy to point the finger
Noting how others mess up real bad
I'm glad I'm not as bad as they are
I could even say I am a little glad

To point at others and their lives
Can make me feel good too
Why look at me I didn't slip
I am so much better than you!

Mama used to say to us
Don't use that pointer finger
Don't compare yourself to others
No telling stories that may linger

I'd like to think I'm perfect
Even though I know I'm not

Whisper Jesus

I'd like to pretend I'm flawless
But then Jesus knows my lot

He sees me when I'm pointing
That silly finger of mine
He knows when I'm being foolish
He sees when I'm not being kind

So once again I come to You
Sweet Jesus wipe my sins away
Cleanse my accusing attitude
Help me listen to what You say

You are the Great Example
The one to Whom I should compare
To all the silly mind games
The world has to share

If I have to use a pointer
Help me point others to Your love
Your cleansing stream from Calvary
That flows from the Father above.

Thank You Jesus!

Rebecca A. Keefe
April 23, 2012

<u>The Valley of Baca (Weeping)</u>

This year we looked at Psalm 84 as we studied about strength that is found in scripture. Part of Psalm 84 talks about passing through the Valley of Baca (Weeping) and while there making a place of refreshment for the next person who goes through that lonely valley after us. We are not to camp in that valley. Just know that it's a season or a time that we are passing through. My Mama used to quote me an old saying of "This too shall pass". It's good to remember that when you are in that valley of weeping. There is another expression I have heard often this past year. It is: "Pay it forward." In other words, if you have received a blessing or a benefit, "pay it forward" by doing the same for someone else who may be in the same type of circumstance later on. No one wants to go through a valley of weeping for it seems, at the time, the tears may never stop. In the early 1980's this is pretty much how I felt. Going through divorce is a horrible experience. There is a ripple effect that travels far and wide because of it. Divorce affects not only the marriage of the couple, but their children, their family, their friends, their neighbor and on it goes. It is never a done deal. The hurt continues for years in the future. Yet there is hope in our God. He does see us and He hears our cry. As verse 7 says "they go from strength to strength" as they seek a closer view of God. Seeking God also means we stop looking at ourselves. We have changed our focus. It is actually possible to go from strength to strength, taking our strength from Him and not people, places or things as we are prone to do. Grabbing the first bit of comfort for anyone close by, moving closer, Whispering "Jesus, Jesus, Jesus" softly as we travel. Sometimes it takes a while to re-focus - but with His help, we can do just that. God bless you as you strive to move closer to our Lord.

Psalm 84 (NKJ)

1 How lovely is Your tabernacle, O Lord of hosts!

2 My soul longs, yes, even faints for the courts of the Lord; My heart and my flesh cry out for the living God.

3 Even the sparrow has found a home, And the swallow a nest for herself, Where she may lay her young—Even Your altars, O Lord of hosts, My King and my God

4 Blessed are those who dwell in Your house; They will still be praising You. Selah

5 Blessed is the man whose strength is in You, Whose heart is set on pilgrimage.

6 As they pass through the Valley of Baca, They make it a spring; The rain also covers it with pools

7 They go from strength to strength; each one appears before God in Zion.

8 O Lord God of hosts, hear my prayer; Give ear, O God of Jacob! Selah

9 O God, behold our shield, And look upon the face of Your anointed.

10 For a day in Your courts is better than a thousand. I would rather be a doorkeeper in the house of my God than dwell in the tents of wickedness.

11 For the Lord God is a sun and shield; The Lord will give grace and glory; No good thing will He withhold from those who walk uprightly.

12 O Lord of hosts, blessed is the man who trusts in You.

Whisper Jesus

The Valley of Baca
(The Valley of Weeping)

Have you been through the Valley of Weeping?
Where your tears flowed like new fallen rain
Where your heart was tender and broken
Where you felt only loss and great pain

Then come to the Savior's refreshing
Stop and sit at His feet for awhile
Let Him give you the Living Water
As He comforts you my child

He redeems the weak and the weary
Those whose strength is almost gone
He says "Don't pitch a tent" in this place
"Follow me – Let's keep moving on!"

In the wilderness and dry places
He shows us how to dig a deep well
So that we can be refreshed and renewed
Helping others move on and not dwell

It's hard when the valley is dry and dark
And we see no hope close by
Yet in the stillness of our hearts
He wipes the tears from our eyes

It's easy to pitch a tent in sadness
To feel no one cares or understands
It's here that our faith is tested

Whisper Jesus

It's where we view His nail scarred hands

We see that He's gone before us
As he uttered his last dying breath
As He cried to our Father in heaven
Who reached down and raised Him from death

So on our knees we start digging deep
Asking God to pour in our soul
The Living Water that quenches all thirst
As He touches and makes us whole

Thank You Lord that You've gone before us
Tempted in all ways like men
Thank You we have Your strength to lean on
As we trust You again and again

Lift us out of this Valley of Baca
As once again You meet our need
Use us Lord to give Your water to the weary
So they too can be saved and freed

It's Your strength that keeps us going
Your Holy Spirit who comforts our soul
It's Your blood that washes our sins away
As You wash us and make us whole

Thank you Lord we don't have to stay in Baca
As You find a way of escape even now
Wrapping Your loving arms around us
As on our knees we humbly bow

Whisper Jesus

Thank You Sweet Jesus!

Written by: Rebecca A. Keefe
April 1, 2014

The Walls

The story of Nehemiah is truly an example of how God can give his servants favor with those in high authorities and of being in the right place at the right time. In Nehemiah's case it was the king that he had found favor with as a faithful servant even though he was a captive. Nehemiah was brought news of how things were in his homeland and it grieved him greatly. The walls around Jerusalem had been broken down and the city was in huge disrepair. It was a very sad state of affairs indeed. Nehemiah went straight to God for help and asked that the king would listen to his request to help his people. This is a beautiful story of how God used the king to meet Nehemiah's need above and beyond what anyone would ever imagine. He was able to go to Jerusalem and begin the rebuilding process. But there was opposition all along the way from nearby enemies. The Israelites had to have a trowel in one hand and a sword in the other. Not an ideal way to build is it? They had to be on guard every minute of the day and night. They also had to tune out the jeers of their enemies who loved to taunt them. Is it any different today? Shouldn't we still be on guard and keep working though the devil would taunt us and make fun of us? It all boils down to coming to God first, confessing our sins, and then proceed with His determination and dedication planted firmly in our hearts. We are never to go into battle or try rebuilding without the help and guidance of Almighty God. Either we are serious in the Lord's work or we are not. Are we willing to fight and willing to build at the same time like Nehemiah?

I have modeled Nehemiah's prayer many times as I have faced troubling situations asking God to give me favor with those in authority and high places and confessing my sins as well. We need a pure heart to go into battle. He is always faithful to do just that - forgive our sins and give us favor in high places. There are physical walls and spiritual walls that need rebuilding as this poem states. As we trust God to bring us through any and every situation He will honor our trust and faith in Him. Praise the Lord! First though, before tackling the battle we must come confidently and quietly before the King of kings and Lord of lords and simply in prayerful worship Whisper Jesus. He is the One who has the Master Plan.

Nehemiah 1:5-9 (NLT)

Then I said, "O LORD, God of heaven, the great and awesome God who keeps his covenant of unfailing love with those who love him and obey his commands,
listen to my prayer! Look down and see me praying night and day for your people Israel. I confess that we have sinned against you. Yes, even my own family and I have sinned!
We have sinned terribly by not obeying the commands, laws, and regulations that you gave us through your servant Moses.
"Please remember what you told your servant Moses: 'If you sin, I will scatter you among the nations.
But if you return to me and obey my commands, even if you are exiled to the ends of the earth, I will bring you back to the place I have chosen for my name to be honored.'
We are your servants, the people you rescued by your great power and might.
O Lord, please hear my prayer! Listen to the prayers of those of us who delight in honoring you. Please grant me success now as I go to ask the king for a great favor. Put it into his heart to be kind to me."

The Walls

There are walls that should be broken down
To let God's Spirit in
Sometimes we need to build a wall
To keep us safe within

The wall that protects our spirit
Is one that gives us Peace
It's a wall that gives protection
And makes the striving cease

The wall that needs to be broken is a
Barrier between God and me
I need those walls to come tumbling down
As I work on coming to Thee

What is the call of my heart Dear Lord
What passion do I feel?
Please show me what Your desire is
As by Your feet I kneel

I may be content just as I am
But that can always change
For life can change in the blink of an eye
And things can be rearranged

To build up or tear down
Please Jesus, show me the way
Let my heart feel Your heart
Should I go or should I stay?

Whisper Jesus

No wall in my spirit
Dear Lord, is my deep desire
Eyes open – heart tender
Is to what I truly aspire

So which tools do I need to use?
Is it a trowel or a sword?
Do I fight the enemy hand to hand
Or do I battle with the Sword of Your Word?

There is a work to do for You
There is an enemy to hinder it all
I lean on your wisdom and your Grace
As I ponder this theme of The Wall.

Rebecca A. Keefe
May 8, 2012

The Wedding Feast of the Lamb

The study of the book of Revelation, the last book of the Bible, is a daunting task. There are so many gifted authors and theologians who have written volumes explaining the mystery of this beautiful book. The women of Bethany have attempted it two times and we realize that we have only barely scratched the surface.

This poem was inspired by attempting to begin that particular study. I invite you to sit and read this wonderful book because it reveals so much of our risen, powerful and reigning King of kings and Lord of lords. Jesus Christ. Sometimes it seems the more I study, the more questions I have, the more I want to know more, and the more I realize how much I still don't know! This is also when I use my Life Application Bible notes. By referring to the footnotes below the verses I am able to fathom a tiny bit of what is written and how it applies to my life today. It's also a time to simply Whisper Jesus in love and adoration for all is was and is and is to come. Powerful! It's worth the 'attempt' to read. And while you attempt to read this powerful book of Revelation - simply Whisper Jesus.

Revelation 1:3 (NIV)

Blessed is the one who reads the words of this prophecy, and blessed are those who hear it and take to heart what is written in it, because the time is near.

The Wedding Feast of the Lamb

When I read Revelation Nineteen
I am in amazement and awe
My mind cannot fully fathom
The magnitude of the vision John saw

Songs of Victory in Heaven
Shouting Hallelujah!, Amen!
Praise our God all you servants
The least, the greatest, all who fear Him

Blessed are those who are invited
To the Wedding Feast of the Lamb
Words of God that are written in truth
Worshiping Jesus the Great I AM

The Rider on the White Horse
Whose name is Faithful and True
The armies of heaven descending
Victorious for me and for you!

King of kings and Lord of lords
No other so powerful and strong
The enemy and his armies defeated
By the sword of His mouth they are gone!

Hallelujah! Amen! He is Risen
He's victorious in all He will do
He's lifting us out of our darkness
Fighting the battle and winning for you!

Whisper Jesus

God give us eyes to see Your Glory
Lifted high above what we only can see
You are our Rock, our King and our Savior
With a Wedding Feast for those you've set free!

Thank You Jesus!

Rebecca A. Keefe
January 29, 2013

They Came To Jesus

They Came to Jesus is a poem that came to me in the middle of the night. For some reason I woke up thinking about these two people, Bartimaeus and the woman with the issue of blood. People who were in desperate need who wanted to meet Jesus face to face. They were determined. The beggar had to rely on the pity of others. The woman had spent all she had on doctors. There was no one else to help them. All hope was gone. Then they heard about a man called Jesus. They began to have hope stir in their hearts so they pressed closer and shouted louder to be heard. They were going to make contact with Jesus no matter what. The beggar shouted as loud as he could, "Jesus!" "Son of David, have mercy on me!" Those nearby tried to quiet him. And the woman thought if she could only touch the hem of his garment, that would be enough. Just touching Him she would be healed.

So it is with us. Jesus has the answer and Jesus is the answer for us no matter what the need. He encourages us to come with a shout, a whisper or a touch. He promises to meet our every need. Whisper Jesus today and ask Him to come closer to meet your need. Or perhaps you need to be the one who seeks him, stepping out and touching Him or crying with a loud voice "Jesus, Son of David, have mercy on me." No matter how you come - He will meet you where you are.

Mark 10:46-52 (NASB)

46 ....a blind beggar named Bartimaeus, were sitting by the road.
47 When he heard that it was Jesus the Nazarene, he began to cry out and say, "Jesus, Son of David, have mercy on me!"

48 Many were sternly telling him to be quiet, but he kept crying out all the more, "Son of David, have mercy on me!"

49 And Jesus stopped and said, "Call him here." So they called the blind man, saying to him, "Take courage, stand up! His is calling for you."

50 Throwing aside his cloak, he jumped up and came to Jesus.

51 And answering him, Jesus said, "What do you want Me to do for you?" And the blind man said to Him, "Rabboni, I want to regain my sight!"

52 And Jesus said to him, "Go; your faith has made you well." Immediately he regained his sight and began following Him on the road.

Luke 8:43-48 (NASB)

43 And a woman who had a hemorrhage for twelve years, and could not be healed by anyone,

44 came up behind Him and touched the fringe of His cloak, and immediately her hemorrhage stopped.

45 And Jesus said, "Who is the one who touched Me?" And while they were all denying it, Peter said, "Master, the people are crowding pressing in on You."

46 And Jesus said, "Someone did touch Me, for I was aware that power had gone out of Me."

47 When the woman saw that she had not escaped notice, she came trembling and fell down before Him, and declared in the presence of all the people the reason why she had touched Him, and how she had been immediately healed.

48 And He said to her, "Daughter, your faith has made you well; go in peace."

Whisper Jesus

They Came To Jesus

There's a story of Blind Bartimaeus
Who heard Jesus was passing by
Though he was a beggar – cold and dirty
He knew Jesus would hear His cry

So he started shouting "Jesus!"
"Son of David have mercy on me"
Jesus stopped in the midst of the noisy crowd
To touch the man who could not see

The people tried to quiet this man
Just a beggar by the roadway
But Jesus heard his fervent cry
Listened to what he had to say

Above the noise and confusion
Amid the excitement and all
Jesus stopped right there in the midst of the crowd
As He heard Bartimaeus call

He did what the beggar asked Him
Touched his blind eyes so he could see
He opened a new world for this poor man
As He commanded the darkness to flee

A new life, new purpose, new goals
No longer destitute, lost and undone
He persisted until Jesus heard him
Healed of blindness and no longer shunned

Whisper Jesus

The sickly woman with the issue of blood
Bowed low, determined, not proud
To see if she could touch Jesus
Pressed closer against the crowd

She didn't cry loud like Bartimaeus
Over the multitude passing by
"If can touch the hem of his garment"
"He'll heal me I know" was her cry

Jesus heard the cry of the beggar
And He felt the woman's touch
In the midst of noise and confusion
Stopping to heal them was not too much

It is just like that for you and me
We can cry loud or press through the crowd
Jesus hears our heart's cry deep within
Shouting out or not speaking aloud

So come to the Savior, don't delay
Whisper softly or shout His name
He'll hear you as you come to Him
Whether you're blind or crippled or lame

You don't have to be a beggar
Or a sad lady filled with despair
He will heal your sick and dying heart
As He wraps you in His care

Whisper Jesus

So, softly whisper Jesus
Or shout with a voice loud and clear
Our Lord will come and touch you
Healing all your needs as you come near.

" Whispering – Jesus"

Rebecca A. Keefe
July 19, 2014

Things Haven't Changed

Our nation watched in horror as the Boston Bombing took place at the Finish Line of the Boston Marathon in April 2013. Our eyes were glued to the television as we all wondered who could do such a thing. Our hearts went out to the victims and their families as we heard all those stories of death and destruction. It was horrible. As I was once again 'thoughting' I began to write this poem, reminded that every day in our world there is untold misery, war and unholy things happening. As we look at history the thought comes: "Things Haven't Changed." In spite of all the atrocities, there is still nothing that could ever separate us from the love of God. What a Hope we have in Him. As I watched I prayed, "Oh Jesus, we are in such a sad state of affairs today in our world. Save us!" As I watched the events unfold that week all I could do was Whisper Jesus! Perhaps you did too.

Romans 8:38-39 (NLT)

And I am convinced that nothing can ever separate us from his love. Death can't, and life can't. The angels can't, and the demons can't. Our fears for today, our worries about tomorrow, and even the powers of hell can't keep God's love away.
Whether we are high above the sky or in the deepest ocean, nothing in all creation will ever be able to separate us from the love of God that is revealed in Christ Jesus our Lord.

Things Haven't Changed

Wars, Discord, Rumors of Wars
Senseless violence and all

Whisper Jesus

Strikes fear into the heart of man
As we wonder on whom do we call?

Danger is rampant
On our neighborhood street
Who do we steer around
And to whom do we greet?

What's happening Lord?
Why is everything so wrong?
What's the matter with people?
Why the killing of the throng?

It all seems so senseless
There is no peace and no joy
People handle bombs and explosives
As if they were a toy

So who do we trust in our day and age
When everyone looks the same?
We go to the Cross, the wonderful Cross
And look to the One who was slain

Lord, help those who are hurt
By this shame and deep despair
Renew their strength completely
Comforting them with Your loving care

Strengthen us, O God like
You did the prophets of old
Renew our will to fight the Enemy

Whisper Jesus

Who is out to destroy our soul

We pray for our nation,
And the world filled with chaos and strife
And we dedicate ourselves to You
Who is the giver of Life

We ask for Your divine wisdom
As we approach each and every day
Save our nation dear Lord above
O hear us when we pray.

Things haven't changed from His day to now
Our enemy knows his days are numbered
Still we stand confident and strong
Facing our Enemy unencumbered

We are more than conquerors. Romans 8

Rebecca A. Keefe
April 21, 2013

Remembering the Boston Bombing Victims of
April 15, 2013

This Is The Day

Did you ever wake up on the wrong side of the bed? Nothing you did turned out right. You spilled coffee on your newly pressed blouse or you dropped your phone into the bathtub or things were just out of sync! When my kids were small the parsonage that we lived in was a large Victorian home that had a servant's stairway going from the kitchen to the second and third floors. When they would stomp into the kitchen in a growly mood, I would say: "Oops, looks like someone got up on the wrong side of the bed! I think you need to go back up to your room and roll over to the other side of the bed and come downstairs with a better attitude." The amazing thing was, they would do just that! Stomp upstairs, hop onto their bed, roll over on the other side and compose them and come down in a better mood. Years later, my son, Cj, said he didn't think they had a choice! If I told them to do it, they did it! Oh if life could be so easy like that again! If, when we find ourselves in a sorry state of mind we could just stomp up to our bedroom and hop on our bed, roll over and get out on the other side with a better attitude. Yet, we can do this in a spiritual sense. If you feel yourself spinning out of control you and I can go to the scripture and read those precious words: "This is the day the Lord has made, I will rejoice and be glad in it." And then, by extreme effort sometimes, we can say out loud: "This is the day the Lord has made – Lord God in heaven – please come into my kitchen, my car as I'm driving, my laundry room, my cubicle at work – help me by your grace to turn this day around and praise you." Does it work? Yes, it does. But it's a choice we have each day. We can also quiet our spirit by simply whispering "Jesus." Not just once, but with head bowed, eyes closed, Whisper Jesus. You will be amazed at the difference it will make in your day. Your attitude will change. It's like going back up the bedroom, hopping on your bed - rolling over to the other side and getting out with a better, improved attitude. All better! It's a choice.

Psalm 118:24 (NLT)

This is the day the LORD has made. We will rejoice and be glad in it.

This Is the Day

This is the day the Lord has made
No matter what comes my way
This is the day the Lord has made
No matter what people say
This is the day the Lord has made
Whether I feel happy or feel sad
This is the day the Lord has made
Whether I am joyful or really mad
This is the day the Lord has made
I have a choice to make today
This is the day the Lord has made
Do I feel sorry for myself or do I pray?
This is the day the Lord has made
Whether I am weak or fit
This is the day the Lord has made
So I'll lift my heart and rejoice in it

Rebecca A. Keefe
January 22, 2013

<u>This One Thing I Know</u>

What a wonderful gift we have in Christ Jesus! As we studied about the covenants in our Ladies Bible Study, it became so much clearer about the price that was paid for our sins. So much is involved in forming a covenant. It was and is a solemn binding agreement. Not to be taken lightly. I truly do not claim to understand the marvelous grace of our precious Lord, but this one thing I know: the Word of God clearly states that my name is written on the palm of His hand. He died for me and for you. No words can ever describe His love for us. And I do know from personal experience when I find a quiet place, settle down and breathe, and simply whisper "Jesus," He is there. He does so much more than we can ever ask of Him. Much like the apostle John writes: John 21:25- Jesus did many other things as well. If every one of them were written down, I suppose that even the whole world would not have room for the books that would be written. (NIV)

Isaiah 49:16 (NASB)

"Behold, I have inscribed you on the palms of my hands

John 15: 13-17 (NASB)

Greater love has no one than this that one lay down his life for his friends. You are my friends if you do what I command
No longer do I call you slaves, for the slave does not know what his master is doing; but I have called you friends, for all things that I have heard from my Father I have made known to you.

You did not choose me but I chose you, and appointed you that you would go and bear fruit, and that your fruit would remain, so that whatever you ask of the Father in my name He may give to you. 17. This I command you, that you love one another:

Isaiah 62:5 (NASB)

And as the bridegroom rejoices over the bride, so your God will rejoice over you.

This One Thing I Know

I don't claim to understand it all
But this one thing I know
Calvary was put in place for me
Where the blood of Christ did flow

A New Covenant was written in His blood
That I may be made clean and whole
He wrote my name on the palm of His hand
Paid the price and saved my soul

He calls me friend no longer a slave
As He laid down His life for me
Forgave my sin and made me new
Opened my eyes that I might see

I don't claim to understand it all
But I accept His Mercy and Grace
For without His sacrifice on the cross
I'd be lost from this human race

Whisper Jesus

The Lamb's Book of Life records my name
It's what the Bible says about me
The angels rejoice when I come to Him
It's recorded for all those who see

There are so many stories in the Bible
Of those who have gone before
Their struggles and trials that were real
Their victories and the armor they wore

May I be found worthy to bear Your Name
As I travel this life here below
May I bring honor and glory to You alone
Sharing Christ so that others may know

A solemn binding agreement
Covenant signed in blood and sacrifice
Not for a day or a week or a month
It's forever that You paid the price

A robe of righteousness I now can wear
The New Covenant makes it so
You took on my sin; I take on Your name
"Little Christ" as I come and go

This one thing I know for sure
Jesus loves me now and forever
The Bible tells me of His love
And that He will leave me – Never!

Thank You Jesus!

Whisper Jesus

Rebecca A. Keefe
February 11, 2014

Thoughting - For Mother's Day

This 'thoughting' is dedicated to all the moms out there, whether you are a mom by adoption or biologically or a spiritual mom to others. May God Bless you!

Exodus 20:12 (NLT)

Honor your father and mother. Then you will live a long, full life in the land the LORD your God will give you.

Psalm 118:24 (NLT)

This the day the LORD has made. We will rejoice and be glad in it.

Rejoice in Him because He loves you and me with an everlasting and eternal Love!

For Mother's Day
Exodus 20:12

Honor your father and mother.
Then you will live a long, full life in the land
the LORD your God will give you.

Even though some of us may not be
a Mother in the sense of having
a child we can call our own,
we still can all lay claim to
having a Mother.

Life is not perfect by any means,

233

Whisper Jesus

And if you are one of those who
do not have happy memories of
a loving Mother
God promises His love that will
encompass and surround us
completely filling in any void places

He is the giver of life
He is the healer of wounds
He is the One who takes the
Brokenness of this world
And mends broken hearts
And increases love among us
He is the eternal God
Whose love never fails.

If you are a Mother and you
Have blessed memories of a
Wonderful mother – then rejoice
With a thankful heart.

We have much to be thankful for.
God is so good.

Celebrate this day
Because it is the Day the
Lord Has Made.

Happy Mother's Day!
May 2013

Whisper Jesus

Rebecca A. Keefe

'Thoughting' Again About a Funeral

Do you think about what others may say when you pass away? I think most of us do. Or maybe it's just the vainness in me that hopes they will say good things! I've often told my kids I hope they tell some corny jokes, referred to in our family as Becky Jokes. What can I say? I love silly, goofy jokes. Whenever I hear one I will call a family member and start out the conversation with: "So anyway, the funny bunny is hopping along in a green speckled field........" and after telling them some silliness they will tell me how bad it is and I should be shot, all done in the spirit of fun. Yet, on the serious side of things, it behooves each of us to leave a good legacy. One that points to Christ and a life lived for Him. When my Mom passed she said she wanted a celebration. She also wanted written on her headstone the words: "Hallelujah, Praise God, I'm Home!" That exactly what she got! She was Home with Jesus, her sincere last wish. What do you want written on your headstone? To me, it really doesn't matter as long as my name is written in the Lamb's Book of Life. But then again – perhaps they could write simply "Lover of God" on my headstone. That would sum up who I am. "Lord Jesus we could shout Your name from the mountain tops because our hearts are filled with love. Still, we can quietly come to You as well and simply Whisper Jesus, knowing You are the Giver of Peace and Diving Love. We are so unworthy of Your great Love, but we are oh so grateful! Sweet Jesus we whisper day I love You. Thank You for loving me!"

John 3:16-17 (NLT)

235

Whisper Jesus

For God so loved the world that he gave his only Son, so that everyone who believes in him will not perish but have eternal life. God did not send his Son into the world to condemn it, but to save it.

'Thoughting' Again About a Funeral

Today we attended a funeral
Of a friend who had passed away
It was a solemn gathering
Listening to what the people had to say

He was a man who loved his family
His God and his fellow man
He leaves behind a legacy
Of one who was led by God's own hand

Then we hear of a cousin passing
Reminded again that life is short
The way we live and the words we say
Leave a legacy for others' report

We sit and we look at the casket
Knowing we soon shall pass this way
Pondering our own soon passing
Wondering what the people will say

We have a Hope in Jesus
This life is not all there is
He forgives our past misfortunes
And lets us know we are His

Whisper Jesus

This wonderful life eternal
Is promised to all who believe
I know Jesus as my Savior
I hope you too will receive

Rebecca A. Keefe
November 20, 2012

<u>To God Be the Glory</u>

This poem was written as I struggled to give a family relationship gone bad to God; trying to resolve an issue where no matter how hard I tried to reconcile it, the worse it got. The more I tried to fix things and understand what was happening, the more misunderstanding of my intent was magnified. It was a battle in my spirit to turn it over to God because I wanted to justify myself. Family! They can drive us crazy or bless us to no end. Eventually, after a lot of angst on my part I was finally able, with His help, to give it to God. This did not happen overnight. It took months to give it to God and let it go. Thanking God in the process that He hears my prayers and He sees my struggles and He will work it all out for His honor and glory.

My Mama used to teach us to glorify the Lord as we prayed and always commit our cares to Him! I am sure she was familiar with the apostle Paul who wrote in Philippians 4:6 (NLT) "Don't worry about anything; instead, pray about everything. Tell God what you need, and thank him for all he has done." She always began her prayers with "Precious Heavenly Father, we love you and thank you for your goodness." It was a good example, one that I try to follow. So why not give that relationship over to the Lord whispering His name softly "Jesus" And trust Him with the outcome. You will never regret letting Him handle the situation.

2 Chronicles 20:15 (NIV)

....This is what the LORD says to you: Do not be afraid or discouraged because of this vast army. For the battle is not yours, but God's.

Psalm 24:8 (NIV)

Who is this King of glory? The LORD strong and mighty, the LORD mighty in battle.

This poem pretty much speaks for itself. The battle is the Lord's, not ours. Thank You Jesus!

To God Be the Glory

To God be the glory for
Battles fought and victories won
To Him be the honor for
For all He has done

Taking my frail nature
My insecurities and all
Redeeming my life daily
As I answer to His call

When I finish the battle
And stand on victory's shore
I know the enemy's regrouping
Not just one battle but more

In myself I don't want to struggle
Yet You tell me to be aware

Whisper Jesus

We have an enemy who is on the prowl
Who is willing to set a snare?

Yes, we do have an adversary
Who is out to steal our soul
But we also have a Redeemer
Who has died to make us whole

Even though I may not want to fight
You lift up my weary arms
You promise through Blood of the Lamb
You will keep me from all harm

So today I give you honor and praise
My weakness is used for Your glory
Enable me Lord to give you the credit
As I share Your wonderful story

You use the small and simple things
To show Your mighty power
Let me never forget it's All About You
Every day and every hour

Make it so, Lord Jesus

Rebecca A. Keefe

October 22, 2013

Watchful Waiting

I suppose watchful waiting could mean being alert, expecting something to happen, watchfully waiting for a loved one to arrive, watchfully waiting for labor pains to begin anticipating the birth of a baby, watchfully waiting for an answer to prayer, watching waiting. Patience, sober, serious, happy, slowly anticipating something to happen soon. Or watchful waiting for a soldier might mean to be alert for the enemy who may be close at hand, alert, vigilant and ready. I don't believe many of us like that waiting part. At least I know I don't! In our instant society we want it now! Yet Jesus tells us to Watch and Wait for His coming. We are admonished to be alert.

"Help us Lord, to watch with our eyes wide open and to be ready! To be watchful knowing that we have an enemy and his name is Satan. I know You want us to be vigilant, and ready and alert. Help us Lord, to be watchful and waiting and faithful!"

Many times as I see the world in extreme chaos everywhere I whisper "Even so, Lord Jesus, come quickly."

Hebrews 13:29, 32,33,34,37 (NASB)

Even so, you too, when you see these things happening recognize that He is near, right at the door.
But of that day or hour no one knows, not even the angels in heaven, nor the Son, but the Father alone.
Take heed, keep on the alert; for you do not know when the appointed time will come.

Whisper Jesus

It is like a man away on a journey, who upon leaving his house and putting his slave in charge, assigning to each on his task, and commanded the doorkeeper to stay on the alert.
What I say to you I say to all, "Be on the alert!" (Watchful waiting)

Watchful Waiting

Watchful Waiting is a term I just heard
I'm pondering what it could mean
To proceed with caution not full speed ahead
When things are not as they seem

I do not like the waiting part
I want things to happen right now
I do not like the watchful part
It means I have to be alert somehow

Yet, that's what we do as we wait for You
As we see signs of the times come true
We are watchful as we read Your Word
As we echo those words anew

Even so – Come Quickly Lord Jesus

Rebecca A. Keefe
July 21, 2012

We Never Know

This poem was written for a dear friend of mine who left home to go shopping. She left her husband home in good health. When she returned she found him dead of a heart attack. No warning. No indication that her life would change drastically that day. Life was good. When she said goodbye that morning she had no idea that it would be the last time she would see her husband alive. We forget that every day is a gift. What we hold near and dear can slip away at any time. Not that we should live in fear. But we should live with a grateful and thankful heart knowing that all we have is a blessing from our loving God above. My husband Francis and I try never to leave the house without telling each other "I love you." Whenever something like a sudden death happens, it is such a devastating surprise. It causes one to think of what is happening in the here and now and what is important and what isn't worth risking a relationship. My daughter Jennifer and her husband Kevin Lindgren are parents of three teenagers. In the awesome task of raising teens, and the gazillion situations that confront them daily with their teenagers, they ask one another the question: "Is this a hill worth dying on?" I think that is a good philosophy to have. What hill are you willing to die on and what battles are willing to let go? Sometimes we can win a battle like that saying goes - and lose the war. You may be like my friend who left her house thinking she was only to be gone a little while and then she and husband would go and does something fun for the day. We never know.

Whatever happens, we are assured in His Word that He never will leave us nor forsake us. No matter what the circumstance. How blessed we are. Still in that time - no matter the circumstance -

we can Whisper Jesus. He can calm every troubled heart just by the mention of His sweet and powerful name. "Jesus"

Hebrews 13:5b & 6 (NASB)

5....."I will never desert you, nor will I ever forsake you,"
so that we confidently say "The Lord is my helper, I will not be afraid." ....

We Never Know

We never know when we say goodbye
If I will see you again
Chances are I will see you soon
And be greeted by your grin

But what if when I leave the house
And you should pass away
Would I have said all I want to you
Or would I leave much more to say

Each day is precious we are told
A gift from God on high
He gives us breath and joy and peace
As He bids us to draw nigh

What if we ignore the signs
That life is growing short
We go on our merry little way
With joking and retorts

Whisper Jesus

To forget to say I love you
I appreciate all you do
Letting each day pass without notice
Of those who love you too

So here's a little reminder
Take a minute more often to say
I love you more than life itself
You mean more to me each day

Thank our precious Lord and Savior
For the gift of His dear Son
For helping us fight the battles
Showing us victories can be won

For it's by His grace we're surviving
All the things life throws our way
And He shows us grace and mercy
An example of what to say

By His grace we love one another
By His love we forgive and go on
We never know what will happen
Let's redeem the day 'er it's gone

Rebecca A. Keefe
April 9, 2013

What I Can Do For You

2 Samuel, Chapter 7 records God's Promise to King David who wanted to build a temple for God. Yet God surprised him and said in essence, "it's not what you can do for me, but what I can do for you". God has so much more in store for us than we could ever dream or think. This poem is what I feel the Lord could be saying to each one of us. It's not so much what we can do for Him, but what He can do for us - has done for us - and will yet do for us. We have no idea of His unlimited power and love. Let me encourage you to sit down and read 2 Samuel Chapter 7. It is a beautiful story. David wanted to do something special for God because he loved Him, but God blew him out of the water so to speak with what His plans were for him instead. It is a wonderful promise to David that extends to us today through Jesus Christ who comes from the line of David. Fantastic! This poem is what I could imagine God is speaking to us. He has so much more in store for us than we can ever imagine. Sit still for a while today, focus on Him and His great love for you. Whisper Jesus and in doing so you may just catch a glimpse of His great love for you.

Ephesians 3:20 (KJV)

Now unto him that is able to do exceeding abundantly above all that we ask or think, according to the power that worketh in us,

What I Can Do For You

It's not so much what you'll do for Me
But what, I, for you, will do
Before the universe was set in place

Whisper Jesus

I had a plan in mind for you

The way to show your love for Me
Is to follow what I say
Bringing all your cares to Me
As I listen while you pray

Even though I know your faults
I love you even still
There's so much more than you'll ever know
As you obey my will

I haven't brought you this far
To let you go on alone
I'm right here close beside you
As My way to you is shone

It's not what you can do for Me
It's what I have done for you
Amazing and unending Love
Strong and faithful and true

Eye has not seen nor has ear heard
Things prepared for those I love
My hand is not shortened nor my ear deaf
To your cries to Your Father above

I am the Giver of all good things
I am the One who calls your name
Relax, stay steady, and come to Me
My love for you stays the same.

Whisper Jesus

My love is unending steadfast and true
My gifts far outweigh your tasks
It's not so much what you do for Me
But what I'll do for thee if you ask

Rebecca A. Keefe
March 29, 2012

What Is A Mother?

I know many women who long to be a mother. Women who would love to have a child that they gave birth to. Yet despite all their prayers and longings, this is one prayer has not come true. I have also seen two reactions. Bitterness and grief mixed in together, acceptance with resolve. Those who have accepted the fact that biologically they cannot birth a baby have become a mom to the orphans, a foster mom, a spiritual mom who can mentor others and become valuable in the role that is available to them. Bitterness and grief are robbers. Here again, it boils down to choice doesn't it? Can you be a mother to someone who is not biologically yours? In my opinion, the answer is yes. Can you become bitter and mad at God for not allowing you to be a mom? Again, in my opinion, the answer is yes. One thing is for certain – we all have a mother! So in my thinking thoughts "thoughting" about mothers, I wrote this poem. "What Is a Mother?"

What Is a mother?

Once a year we give special honor
To women both great and small
Who've given birth or adopted a baby
Or seem like a Mother to all

So, is a Mom just a simple lady?
Who wipes the tears away
Or is she an angel sent from heaven
To teach her children how to pray

Jesus had a Mother too

Whisper Jesus

Who kept God's Word in her heart?
She watched Him grow in strength and love
And saw Him miracles impart

As women they are gifted
With an impenetrable love
That hangs on through thick and thin
And is given from God above

A Mother's love is unshakeable
It's steady, strong and true
She loves her own no matter what
And will always see them through

She has to be tough and unbending
In matters where it counts
But she can also bring laughter and joy
When the young and old want to pout

So, what is a Mother?
She's a lady, a comfort, a friend
She knows how to and encourage
Knowing some problems will have an end

She gives her child to Jesus
Asks that He guide them all their lives
She carries their sorrows and their joys
Asking God's blessings to make them thrive

But there is no child of her own to love
She devotes herself to the orphan

Whisper Jesus

She adopts and rescues the weary ones
Giving to those who've been overcome

A Mother is so many things
Lover, sister, aunt, and friend
Daughter, wife, worker, and cook
Her value and gifts seem to have no end

She's a kisser of boo boos and broken hearts
From infants to grown up kids
And she points her loved ones to Jesus
Knowing His love – He never forbids

Lord, please bless all the Mothers
Showing them Your love is faithful and true
Bless their lives with strength and power
No matter what valley they go through

Shower our Moms with determination
To never give up or give in
Watch over her family great or small
Grant her many victories in You to win!

Make it so Lord Jesus!
Mother's Day 2014

Rebecca A. Keefe

When I Couldn't Love Myself

Isn't it wonderful that God loves us to such a great extent as the scriptures declare! We are not left to save ourselves. God has already taken care of that. Today I invite you to read His precious Word called the Holy Bible - think about it, then think about it some more. Mull it over in your mind. Write it down, look at it, read it out loud, then think about it some more. Read it in different versions and translations. When I couldn't love myself, Jesus already loved me and that makes life worth living! For even if I can't love myself, that never negates the fact that we need to hear that Jesus loves me over and over. For years we have sung the children's song, "Jesus loves me this I know, for the Bible tells me so." It portrays a truth beyond our comprehension! We just need to believe it. A phrase that was popular several years ago was: "God said it, I believe it, that settles it." It is through and by the Name of Jesus that we experience His sweet love. When I couldn't love myself – He loved me then, He loves now, He will love me forever! "As I softly whisper Your name - Jesus - let my faith soar heavenward and grasp that fact that You do indeed love me! Sweet Jesus I love you and praise You that You love me!"

John 3:16-17 (NLT)

For God so loved the world that he gave his only Son, that everyone who believes in him will not perish but have eternal life.
God did not send his Son into the world to condemn it but to save it.

Whisper Jesus

When I Couldn't Love Myself

When I couldn't love myself
My Jesus loved me still
He gave His life that I might live
Because it was God's will

He cares much more than I could care
He loves me, this I know
He cleans me up and sets me straight
Erases all my woes

To pay the debt for all my sin
To rise and live again
Is more than I can imagine
Though I deserve judgment and chagrin

My name is written in The Lamb's Book of Life
When my sins are wiped away
He takes my weak and stubborn heart
Puts His love in me to stay

I'm the one who's moved away
When I take my eyes off Him
He moves in close to hear my prayer
When I confess to Him my sin

When I couldn't love myself
He paid the price for me

253

Whisper Jesus

Instead of condemnation
He came to set me free

I'm so prone to do 'my thing'
Forgetting His way is best
But he shows me over and over
His Love always meets the test

No matter how far I stray from Him
His love follows me always
His thoughts and ways much higher than mine
In the end I'm always amazed

Jesus loves me This I know
For the Bible tells me so
Come with me as I follow Him
Sharing His love to all we know.

Make it so, Lord Jesus

Rebecca A. Keefe
June 11, 2013

<u>When I Think About The Cross</u>

The Cross, in reality, is a gruesome, ugly sight. I don't like to think about all the suffering and agony that is endured when an execution such as death on the cross portrays. Yet, it is because of the Cross that we have been adopted into the family of God. I would rather think about the pleasant things that Jesus did, healing the sick, raising the dead, putting children on his knee, comforting the grieving. These are all things that do not involve agony, death and despair. But the Cross was all part of God's plan, the good as well as the bad. It was for me and you. We should never take lightly the sacrifice that was paid for our sins. What a marvelous Hope we have because of the Cross. Hallelujah! "Jesus" "Just the mention of Your name causes devils to flee, storms to cease and peace to reign. I will simply Whisper Jesus and praise You for Your great sacrifice."

Isaiah 53 (NIV)

1 Who has believed our message and to whom has the arm of the Lord been revealed?

2 He grew up before him like a tender shoot, and like a root out of dry ground. He had no beauty or majesty to attract us to him, nothing in his appearance that we should desire him

3 He was despised and rejected by mankind, a man of suffering, and familiar with pain. Like one from whom people hide their faces he was despised, and we held him in low esteem.

4 Surely he took up our pain and bore our suffering, yet we considered him punished by God, stricken by him, and afflicted.

5 But he was pierced for our transgressions, he was crushed for our iniquities; the punishment that brought us peace was on him, and by his wounds we are healed.

6 We all, like sheep, have gone astray, each of us has turned to our own way; and the Lord has laid on him the iniquity of us all.

7 He was oppressed and afflicted, yet he did not open his mouth; he was led like a lamb to the slaughter, and as a sheep before its shearers is silent, so he did not open his mouth.

8 by oppression and judgment he was taken away. Yet who of his generation protested? For he was cut off from the land of the living; for the transgression of my people he was punished.

9 He was assigned a grave with the wicked, and with the rich in his death, though he had done no violence, nor was any deceit in his mouth.

10 Yet it was the Lord's will to crush him and abuse him to suffer, and though the Lord makes his life an offering for sin, he will see his offspring and prolong his days, and the will of the Lord will prosper in his hand.

11 After he has suffered, he will see the light of life and be satisfied; by his knowledge my righteous servant will justify many, and he will bear their iniquities.

12 Therefore I will give him a portion among the great, and he will divide the spoils with the strong, because he poured out his life unto death, and was numbered with the transgressors. For he bore the sin of many, and made intercession for the transgressors

John 3:16 & 17 (NIV)

16 For God so loved the world that He gave His one and only Son that whoever believes in Him shall not perish but have eternal life

17 For God did not send His Son into the world to condemn the world, but to save the world through him.

When I Think About The Cross

When I think about the Cross
Where my Savior hung and died
As He took on all my guilt and sins
Where He was beaten and crucified

It makes my whole heart tremble
As I see His suffering and pain
And I know without His sacrifice
I would not have heaven to gain

I'd rather think about the children
That He sat upon His knee
And watch the lame man walk and run
And the blind man begin to see

I'd rather listen to the stories
Of how He calmed the mighty storm
How He stilled the waves and winds
As the waters He transformed

He fed the thousands on the hills
As they swarmed to hear His teaching
They loved to hear His words so sweet
Never tiring of His preaching

To think this Man would give His life
Was the farthest thing from their mind
Yet that is why He came to earth
Becoming a sacrifice for all mankind

Whisper Jesus

I'd rather think of the pleasant things
His disciples and their fishing
Telling them – cast their nets on the other side
And they'd see what they'd been missing

Yet the Cross was there in God's great plan
That He should die for you and me
That He should rise again on that third day
Defying death – just to set us free

So when I think about the Cross
It's not just with sadness, sorrow and woe
It's with joy for my salvation
Knowing He's conquered my every foe

Because of Him I am free from sin
Free from all guilt and despair
Because of Him I have a Heavenly Hope
As a partaker of His love I share

So as I think upon the Cross
I rejoice because it doesn't end there
He'll come again to catch us away
And we'll meet Him in the air.

Thank You Sweet Lord Jesus!

Rebecca A. Keefe
Easter April 2014

<u>Who or What is King</u>

The Word of God is full of stories of simple men who trusted God with all their hearts despite overwhelming odds. Just look at the Old Testament. It is filled with stories of battles won by unusual means. Not mighty armies or well-armed troops. There were men like Gideon, Joshua, Moses, David and many more. It is truly by the grace of God that battles are won.

I am reminded of Ecclesiastes 9:11 where it states ....The race is not to the swift or the battle to the strong, nor does food come to the wise or wealth to the brilliant or favor to the learned; but time and chance happen to them all. God only asks that we trust Him fully and try not to figure things out on our own. His way is always best. When things are going well, I may think it is all my doing, until I stop and recognize that God is blessing me. Who is King of my life and my heart? As I sit and whisper quietly the name of Jesus, I recognize once again that His Name is the Name above all other names.

Who or What is King

False modesty says there's no question
I have no King but Jesus alone
Nothing rules my emotions or desires
And towards sin I am never prone

To suggest such a thing is a silly lie
My sinful nature comes forefront and first
David prayed Search My Heart O Lord
As he asked God to quench his thirst

Whisper Jesus

Who is my King in my spiritual life?
Who do I give credit to?
Am I apt to give all the glory to me?
And leave His Name out of view

I come to God in desperation
Ask His Help in my time of need
I promise Him all kinds of allegiance
As upon His Name I plead

Then the need is met and resolved
Life turns back to normal again
Am I like the lepers who never gave thanks?
Or do I give Him glory for all I have gained

Do I deflect the glory back to God?
Or do I give the credit solely to me
Like it was all my brains and intellect
That finally set me free

Am I keeping what belongs to God?
Cause if I do it becomes a snare
Help me Jesus to give Glory to You
As You all my burdens share

I ask you Lord for forgiveness
For keeping things that belong to You
Help me to humbly walk before You
In all I say and do

Whisper Jesus

I want to have a heart like David
And courage like Gideon of old
Show me the idols I keep for myself
And only give me a heart of gold

Forgive me for doing things on my own
For not giving You both joy and sorrow
Help me learn from the lessons in Your Book
Let it be Mercy and Grace that I borrow

You show me paths that I never dreamed
How You rescue my fallen estate
How You make a way where there is no way
How Your counsel is never ever late

When I get puffed up with my own importance
The credit is not mine to save face
Not my might not my power has conquered the odds
It's All by Your Power and Grace.

Make it so, Lord Jesus

Rebecca A. Keefe
October 15, 2013

Within This Circle

There is a story told of an evangelist of old, who upon entering a new town to preach the Gospel would draw a circle on the ground. He would then step inside this circle and begin to pray that revival would begin within that circle and within his own heart and soul. He knew his preaching would be useless unless he was in right standing with God. To bring this illustration home I brought in a large hula-hoop to the ladies Bible study. One of the ladies had graciously loaned one to me that was very colorful. I placed the hula-hoop on the floor and related the story of the evangelist who prayed for revival to start within his circle. I invited them to do the same for their neighborhood, their children, their town and community. We often forget that if the revival fires aren't burning brightly in our own hearts and souls, the love of God cannot be clearly seen by others. "Lord, I draw a circle around me today and I ask by Your grace and mercy that You begin a work in me. In this circle also, I simply whisper Your Name "Jesus" and believe that you are able to do exceedingly abundantly more than I can ask or think. Thank you!"

Ephesians 3:20 (NLT)

Now glory be to God! By his mighty power at work within us, he is able to accomplish infinitely more than we would ever dare to ask or hope.

Isaiah 40:31 (KJV)

But they that wait upon the Lord shall renew their strength; they shall mount up with wings as eagles; they shall run and not be weary; and they shall walk and not faint.

Whisper Jesus

Within This Circle

I draw a circle on the ground
And put myself inside
In this circle that I stand
I ask You to abide

To change me first I ask You now
Not others whose faults I see
I want you Lord to change them
But most of all, change me

I want revival in my town
My family, my friends, my foes
But with You I have to be honest
I need You in my head, my heart, my toes

All of me, dear Lord I pray
No part of me left unclean
Wash me with Your Precious Blood
Even the sins that appears unseen

Within this circle that I stand
Begin a work in me
With no excuses that I give
Of all malice and sin, set me free

A heart of love and caring
Comes from You and You Alone
I have no goodness in myself
Only from You with sins atoned

Whisper Jesus

So in this circle that I've drawn
Help me reach up to only Thee
And remind me I cannot reach others
Until it's You only that I see

I know in my heart I am nothing
Yet your Word shows the opposite is true
Your wisdom and Your counsel
Show great things can be done through You

You speak the Word into our hearts
You empower us to do your will
You unite us together as we meet
Against the enemy while serving you still

So here in this circle that I stand
It's just between me and You
Help me show the Love of Jesus
In all I say and do

Make it so Lord Jesus,
Amen

Rebecca A. Keefe
August 2013

Words

My sister, Martha Gregor, has often quoted the phrase: "Least said, most easily mended." It is well worth thinking about since our tongue is the part of our anatomy that gets us in trouble most often. One of the gals in the Bible study group asked that I write a poem about words. She was having a hard time keeping her mouth shut when things were happening around her that she didn't particularly agree with. When we are passionate about someone or something we can be very out spoken. The words flow very easily. Whether they are good words or bad words is not taken into account at the time. All we know is, we feel we just have to say something! This poem is just a little reminder about Words. One of the sweetest, most powerful words we can say however is the Name of Jesus. Whisper Jesus. Calm down, breathe in, breathe out, then quietly and reverently whisper the almighty name of Jesus.

James 3:1-5 & 8-10 (NLT)

Not many of you should presume to be teachers, my brothers, because you know that we who teach will be judged more strictly.
We all stumble in many ways. If anyone is never at fault in what he says, he is a perfect man, able to keep his body in check.
When we put bits into the mouths of horses to make them obey us, we can turn the whole animal.
Or take ships for example. Although they are so large and are driven by strong winds, they are steered by a very small rudder wherever the pilot want to go.
Likewise the tongue is a small part of the body, but it makes great boasts.

but no man can tame the tongue. It is a restless evil, full of deadly poison.

With the tongue we praise our Lord and Father, and with it we curse men, who have been made in God's likeness.

Out of the same mouth come praise and cursing. My brothers, this should not be.

Words

Less said, most easily mended,
Than saying too much
and my friend is offended

The power of words
Can bring nations to fight
Yet a sweet Word from God
Can make anger take flight

Do I cause pain
Or do my words mend
Do my words bring peace
Or do I offend

The tongue is mighty
Like a rudder on a ship
It can build great armies
Or cause someone to slip

To speak my mind
Of that I am quite good
With only me to blame

Whisper Jesus

If I am misunderstood

You see, Lord, my problem
Is myself and I and me!
So I ask you to take this silly tongue
And let it glorify only Thee!

Rebecca A. Keefe
June 26, 2012

Who is This?

As kids we'd listen to the radio with The Lone Ranger and Tonto. People would ask: "Who was that masked man?" We had an old radio that had a wire attached to it for antennae - and since I was the youngest, my two older brothers, Dayne and Frankie would make me hold the antennae. If I held it just right the sound would come in perfect, sounds strange but it was true. There was always a rescuer on television or the movies, someone to come in at the last minute and rescue the one in distress. How exciting! But those were made believe stories, fictional characters. They looked good on paper. Today's poem is about someone who looks good and can act good even on a stormy sea. It's about someone who cares for you and me in real life. He is the same yesterday, today and forever. And He is someone I can trust with all my yesterdays and my today and my tomorrows. If you haven't thought about this someone and would like to know Him, it is so simple to come to Him. He is your Redeemer and Friend. His name is Jesus. All you have to do is softly whisper His Name. "Jesus." He will come to your rescue - I guarantee it!

John 3:16-17 (NLT)

For God so loved the world that he gave his only Son, so that everyone who believes in him will not perish but have eternal life. God did not send his Son into the world to condemn it, but to save it.

Who Is This?

Who is this who can
Calm a stormy sea?

268

Whisper Jesus

Who is this who can
Speak to even me?

Who is this who
Carries all my cares?
Who is this who
All my sorrow shares?

Who is this who numbers
The hairs upon my head?
Who is this who raises
People from the dead?

Who is this who casts
All my sins away?
Who is this who is
In my life to stay?

Oh! Who is this Jesus?
God's own dear precious Son
Who defeated Death on Calvary
And all our battles won

Who is this Man who is
Coming back again?
Jesus! My dear Savior
My Redeemer – My dearest Friend!

Rebecca A. Keefe
September 25, 2012

You Make All Things Work Together

God has a way of turning things around when all hope seems lost. He has the power to do that. The frustration in life comes when we keep trying to right the wrongs ourselves, thinking that we are the great fixer-upper instead of Him. When disappointed many times the emphasis zeroes in on me, myself and I - when it should be turned toward Him, Himself on High. He has a way of working things out even when we mess with the plan. That's reason to rejoice and be glad that Christ alone is our anchor and our hope. I am so happy that I am not left alone to work things out for myself! Aren't you? When I get the breath knocked out of me by life circumstances, it makes me stop dead in my tracks. Life has a way of throwing surprises our way when least expected. That's when I stop and try to catch my breath and take it all in. And in doing so, I am reminded to come to Jesus, again. I've often wondered what folks do who don't have Jesus to turn to. His Word is so encouraging and true. Sometimes hard memories have a way of smacking us or we run into a person who hurt us in the past and hurts we thought long forgotten suddenly surface. How do we handle those things? It's when I "stop" - start to breathe again and simply whisper the sweet and powerful Name of Jesus that my confidence is renewed and my courage returns. Sometimes I just whisper "Oh Jesus, You know. Help me wade through this once again, Jesus sweet Jesus".

Romans 8:26-28 (NIV)

In this way, the Spirit helps us in our weakness. We do not know what we ought to pray for, but the Spirit himself intercedes for us with groans that words cannot express.

And he who searches our hearts knows the mind of the Spirit, because the Spirit intercedes for the saints in accordance with God's will.

And we know that in all things God works for the good of those who love, who have been called according to his purpose.

You Make All Things Work Together

You make all things work together
For those who truly love God
Who are called according to Your purpose
Here in this world that we trod

In disappointments, darkness and hurts
You are my Anchor and Hope
In my secret place of prayer
You give me power to cope

Sometimes it seems so heavy
To bear my burdens alone
And yet You never leave me
Reaching down to me from Your throne

I cannot see beyond the bend
Of what may lay ahead
But I know if You walk with me
You remove from me all dread

You ask me to draw closer still
Find that secret place of prayer
To pour my deepest secrets out

Whisper Jesus

As You listen to me there

You have a way of turning things
From the worse to better instead
It's because of Your great sacrifice
And Your precious blood that was shed

So when I'm feeling lonely and tired
Stressed with heaviness that life brings
Remind me You work things together for my good
As You cause my heart to sing

Thank You God for loving me
For forgiving my sins and more
Thank You for my home in heaven
And all You have in store

You make all things work together
Though I may not understand
Yet I'm confident You are with me
As You hold me in the palm of Your hand

So I commit my way unto You
You work it out Your way not mine
Have Your will in my heart and life
And make me totally Thine.

Make it so Lord Jesus!

Rebecca A. Keefe
December 3, 2013

<u>Bibliography/Reference</u>

The Holy Bible Life Application Bible New Living Translation, Tyndale House Publishers, Inc. Wheaton Illinois 1996

The Holy Bible New International Version, Holman Bible Publishers, Nashville, Tennessee. Copyright 1983, 1984

Holy Bible, New American Standard Bible, by the Lockman Foundation, A Corporation Not for Profit, La Habra, CA 2000 Copyright 1960, 1962, 1963, 1968, 1971, 1972, 1973, 1975, 1977, 1995

Holy Bible, King James Version, Tyndale House Publishers, Life Application Bible, 1986, 1988, 1989

Holy Bible, New King James Version, Zondervan Bible Publishers, Copyright 1964, 1972

Dear Reader,

I want to thank you for choosing this book to read. I truly hope it has been and will continue to be a blessing to you. Perhaps you will leave it out on your coffee table and pick it up from time to time. The best way I can thank you is to write a poem just for you. I pray God blesses you richly as we serve Him together.

In His Love and mine,
Rebecca Ann Keefe

I would like to thank you
For picking up this book
My prayer has been sincerely that
You'd be blessed as you take a look

I pray that it will bless you
And challenge you even more
To explore God's Sweet and Wonderful Word
Seeking what He has in store

For He is closer than a brother

Whisper Jesus

He will be Your Forever Friend
He will never ever leave you
He's One on whom you can depend

Thank you also to the friends
In Touch Ladies Bible Group and more
Who encouraged me to write these poems
Sharing God's gift that's not a chore

May God bless you as you read these lines
Encourage you as you pray
Whispering the sweet Name of Jesus
Making Him welcome every single day

Thank you again for reading this book
I pray it has caused you to stop and Whisper His Name
A simple reminder to step closer
Just Whisper Jesus – you will never be the same

In Christ Jesus Our Lord and Savior,
Rebecca Ann Keefe
July 8, 2014

Numbers 6:24-26

The LORD bless you and keep you.
The LORD make his face shine upon you
and be gracious to you.
The LORD turn his face toward you
and give you peace.